FOUNDATIONS

OF

TEACHING

METHOD

FOUNDATIONS

OF

TEACHING

METHOD

John A. Laska
University of Texas at Austin

and

Stanley L. Goldstein
Western Washington State College,
Bellingham, Washington

WM. C. BROWN COMPANY PUBLISHERS
Dubuque, Iowa

Credits

B. F. Skinner, "The Science of Learning and the Art of Teaching," *Harvard Educational Review*, 24, Spring 1954, pp. 86, 87, 90-92, 93-95. Copyright 1954 by President and Fellows of Harvard College.

John Dewey, *Experience and Education* (New York: Macmillan, 1938), pp. 83-85. Used by permission of Kappa Delta Pi, an Honor Society in Education, owners of the copyright.

To: Kristrun

and

To: Elinor
     Nicole
     Kirsten

Contents

Preface

This book is intended for use as a primary or supplementary text in general foundations of education courses, curriculum courses, history of education courses, and educational psychology courses. We believe that one of the principal objectives of these courses is to provide prospective teachers with an understanding of the basic conceptions of teaching method. Our book is designed to facilitate the attainment of that objective by providing a classification of the major views on teaching method and an analysis of the writings of the important educational thinkers who have expressed these views.

Courses in the foundations of education in particular have been criticized sharply in recent years for their alleged failure to be "relevant." But we can conceive of nothing more relevant to a prospective teacher than an appreciation of the foundations of instructional method. The modern professional teacher needs to know *why* certain teaching methods are considered to effective, instead of merely accepting on faith that a particular method is suitable.

We have tried to produce a book which focuses on the views of the major Western educational writers on teaching method. Although many other books have attempted to deal with the views of such eminent educationists as Rousseau and Dewey, these books usually fail to distinguish clearly between the ideas of the educationist on how to make the teaching process more effective from his view on what he thinks should be the goals of education. It is only with the first of these topics that our book is concerned.

We have sought to make an original contribution to an understanding of teaching method. While we recognize that a large assortment of terms has been used to identify instructional methods (activity method, deductive method, expository method, inductive method, discussion method, for example), we are unaware of the existence of a rigorous and systematic classification of teaching methods on the basis of well-defined differentiating characteristics. We must emphasize, however, that our classification is a descriptive one; it is not intended to have theoretical significance at the present time. We have also avoided making a value judgment about any of the methods we have described. Our principal concern is to categorize the methods and to provide an opportunity for the great educational thinkers to speak about them.

We would like to express our sincerest gratitude to Susan German for her exceptional skill and patience in typing the manuscript. Our appreciation is also due to Ana Marie Castro and Linda Engelland for their assistance in the preparation of the manuscript. For many insightful discussions of teaching method, we would like to thank our colleagues William Bailey, Garnet McDiarmid, and James J. Shields, Jr.

John A. Laska
Stanley L. Goldstein

1

Traditional Teaching Methods

The activity that we call teaching has been with us since the earliest times. For thousands of years fathers have taught their sons what they will need to know as adults, and mothers have taught their daughters. Because of the importance to mankind of the teaching process, human beings have also been seeking to improve their methods of teaching. How many fundamentally different methods of teaching have been devised, and what are the characteristics of the basic teaching methods?

Before we attempt to answer the central question of this book, we first need to consider the nature of the teaching process and the factors that are responsible for the fundamental differences among teaching methods.

Nature of the Teaching Process

The basic elements that are found in any teaching situation consist of a teacher, at least one student, and a learning objective that the teacher expects the student to achieve. The problem that the teacher faces is how to get the student to learn. The only way for the teacher to solve this problem is to make use of *stimuli*; these stimuli may come from sources outside the student, or they may originate within the student. For example, the teacher talking to the student or showing him a picture illustrates the use of external stimuli. Internal stimuli include such things as ideas which originate in the mind of the student and cause him to learn or the feelings and interests that the student has which prompt him to make an effort to learn.

What do these stimuli do to bring about learning in the student? The function of some stimuli is to get the student to make an effort to learn; that is, to motivate the student. We shall refer to these stimuli as *effort-producing stimuli*. Once the student is motivated, the function of other stimuli is to control what the student will learn. We shall call these *outcome-shaping stimuli*. Outcome-shaping stimuli cause the student to attain one specific learning outcome rather than another, whereas the function of effort-producing stimuli is to increase the likelihood that the student will learn something.

How Do Teaching Methods Differ?

The reason there are different methods of teaching is that there are different basic assumptions or theories about what is the most effective way to motivate students (the use of effort-producing stimuli)and different basic assumptions about the most effective way to bring about a particular learning outcome (the use of outcome-shaping stimuli). We shall now present a concise overview of these basic theories; they will be elaborated in greater detail in other parts of the book.

Effort-Producing Stimuli.   There are two major theories about the use of effort-producing stimuli in the teaching process.[1] The first is that the student will learn more effectively if the teacher and/or society through the use of aversive techniques openly or overtly tries to induce the student to make an effort to learn. (By "society" we mean parents, school authorities, and governments; by "aversive techniques" we mean placing the student in a situation in which he will suffer unpleasant consequences if he

---

1. Our discussion of motivational theories in this book is for general descriptive and classificatory purposes only. The explanations are not intended to be scientifically rigorous.

does not make an effort to learn; by "openly" or "overtly" we mean that the student is aware that someone wants him to learn.) Under this theory, the student feels that he is being compelled by someone to learn. We shall refer to the type of effort-producing stimulus that is involved in this theory as an *overtly provided, aversive* effort-producing stimulus. The second theory is that the student will learn more effectively if he believes that he is free to decide what and when he should learn. Hence the type of effort-producing stimulus involved in this theory we shall call *student-originated*.

Outcome-Shaping Stimuli. There are also two major theories about the use of outcome-shaping stimuli in the teaching process.[2] The first major theory holds that *before* the student is able to learn, he must receive an appropriate outcome-shaping stimulus. We shall refer to these stimuli as *pre-response* outcome-shaping stimuli. This theory may be further subdivided into two different points of view. The first of these is that student learning will take place with relatively little effort required from the student and with essentially a passive role for the student in the teaching process. For example, it is assumed that a student who listens to a lecture will learn from the lecture. The second point of view is that the student must be relatively active in order to learn and must put forth considerable effort. This second assumption about the need for student activity may in turn be further subdivided. One point of view is that student learning occurs gradually through practice. Another theory is that after a student has made an effort to solve a problem, he will have an experience of insight.

The second major theory about the use of outcome-shaping stimuli assumes that a student will learn only if he receives a reinforcement *after* he makes the desired response. One type of reinforcement consists of the presentation of certain post-response stimuli. For example, if a teacher says "good" after a student has made a correct response, it is expected that the student will be more likely to repeat the response in the future. Another type of reinforcement consists of the post-response removal of certain pre-

2. Our discussion of learning theories in this book is for general descriptive and classificatory purposes only. The explanations are not intended to be scientifically rigorous.

response stimuli. For example, a student may be told by a teacher that he has failed his first course examination. The student, who has thus been made subject to anxiety-provoking stimuli, then studies for the next course examination and is afterwards told that based on his second performance he is no longer failing. It is expected as a result of the removal of the anxiety-provoking stimuli, that he will be more likely in the future to continue the mode of study he used in preparing for his second examination. Although the second type of reinforcement entails the removal of a stimulus rather than the presentation of one, we shall refer to both types of reinforcements as *post-response* outcome-shaping stimuli.

Let us now summarize what we have said about the nature of the teaching process and the fundamental differences among teaching methods. The process of teaching involves a teacher and at least one student. The teacher has a learning objective for the student. In order to accomplish this objective he makes use of two kinds of stimuli: effort-producing and outcome-shaping. Teaching methods may differ because the assumption underlying some methods is that overtly provided, aversive effort-producing stimuli must be used while other methods rest on the assumption that the effort-producing stimuli must be student-originated. With respect to outcome-shaping stimuli, methods may differ on the basis of whether these stimuli should be pre-response or post-response. The methods which depend upon pre-response outcome-shaping stimuli may be further differentiated on the basis of whether the learner is passive or active. And finally, among the conceptions of teaching method which postulate the use of pre-response outcome-shaping stimuli and an active role for the student, one method may rest on the assumption that learning takes place gradually through practice and another that the student learns through insight.

The Traditional Teaching Methods

In the remainder of this chapter we shall consider the three earliest teaching methods developed by mankind. We do not know exactly when these methods were first formulated, but original writings are available which indicate that the ancient Greeks and Romans were familiar with them. We shall refer to these methods as the "traditional" teaching methods.

The methods will first be explained and then documented by selections from representative classical educational writers. Each of the three traditional methods will be identified by our own labels; our terminology is not intended to represent the classification of methods used by the Greco-Roman writers. Nor does our identification of three different methods mean that each of these methods was utilized by teachers only in its "pure" form; as is usually the case today, teachers have probably always tended to use a combination of methods in attaining their instructional objectives.

For the purposes of our classification system, all basic teaching methods are regarded as being mutually exclusive. The classification of borderline cases, therefore, is always a matter of judgment.

Telling/Showing Method: Explanation

The first teaching method to be described we shall call the Telling/Showing Method. This method is based on the following fundamental assumptions: (1) The most effective way of motivating students is to use overtly provided, aversive effort-producing stimuli. (2) The most effective way of achieving the desired learning objective is by using pre-response outcome-shaping stimuli with a relatively passive role for the student and a minimum effort required from the student.

The term "Telling" in the designation for this method refers to the possibility of using verbal stimuli (such as the spoken or written word) as the principal type of outcome-shaping stimulus. The term "Showing" refers to the possibility of using nonverbal experiences (such as touching an object in order to learn about its characteristics). This practice of using two words to identify the method is followed in order to convey a better notion of the range of techniques encompassed by the method (it will also be used in connection with the other two methods described in this chapter). It should be clearly understood, however, that all of these techniques are aspects of the same basic method.

The two alternatives within the Telling/Showing Method of using either verbal or nonverbal experiences have given rise to strong differences of opinion. Those who advocate the use of Telling stress the greater efficiency of verbal stimuli (in a given amount of time, many more ideas can be communicated by symbolic means than through nonverbal experiences). On the other hand, those who favor Showing emphasize the greater impact of direct experience and the possibility that words may be misunderstood, or, even worse, that the student may merely commit the words to rote memory and thus be able to give the appearance of having learned while not having understood their meaning.

Typical examples of the outcome-shaping techniques employed by teachers when they use the Telling/Showing Method are lecturing, presenting films and slides, performing a scientific experiment in front of a class, and taking students on a field trip. Examples of the kinds of motivational techniques that a teacher might employ (for this method and the other two traditional methods) is provided in the following section, which is concerned with the documentation of the method.

Telling/Showing Method: Documentation

In this section (and in a comparable manner elsewhere for the other two traditional methods of teaching) we shall provide documentation from certain Greco-Roman educational writers to establish the existence of a conception of the method during the classical period. The selections which follow are meant to be illustrative only; they are not intended to indicate the extent to which the Telling/Showing Method was actually utilized. We shall confine our excerpts to the following classical writers on education: Isocrates (Greece, 436-338 B.C.), Plato (Greece, 427-347 B.C.), Aristotle (Greece, 384-322 B.C.), and Quintilian (Rome, 35-95 A.D.).

Plato recognized the pervasiveness of the Telling Method:

> Education and admonition commence in the first years of childhood, and last to the very end of life. Mother and nurse and father and tutor are vying with one another about the improvement of the child as soon as ever he is able to understand what is being said to him: he cannot say or do anything without their setting forth to him that this is just and that is unjust; this is honourable, that is dishonour-

able; this is holy, that is unholy; do this and abstain from that.[3]

The use of physical objects to provide nonverbal learning experiences (Showing) is also documented by Plato:

> We must . . . supervise craftsmen of every kind and forbid them to leave the stamp of baseness, licence, meanness, unseemliness, on painting and sculpture, or building, or any other work of their hands; and anyone who cannot obey shall not practise his art in our commonwealth. We would not have our Guardians grow up among representations of moral deformity, as in some foul pasture where, day after day, feeding on every poisonous weed they would, little by little, gather insensibly a mass of corruption in their very souls. Rather we must seek out those craftsmen whose instinct guides them to whatsoever is lovely and gracious; so that our young men, dwelling in a wholesome climate, may drink in good from every quarter, whence, like a breeze bearing health from happy regions, some influence from noble works constantly falls upon eye and ear from childhood upward, and imperceptibly draws them into sympathy and harmony with the beauty of reason, whose impress they take.[4]

The classical writers on education also made reference to the use of overtly provided, aversive effort-producing stimuli (the use of these stimuli applies to the Telling/Showing Method and also to the other two traditional methods of teaching). This procedure is described by Protagoras in Plato's dialogue: "And if he [the child] obeys, well and good; if not, he is straightened by threats and blows, like a piece of bent or warped wood."[5] The use of other motivational techniques was also recognized by classical educational writers. Quintilian, for example, suggested the use of praise and rewards to promote learning: "Let the pupil be asked ques-

---

3. Plato *Protagoras* 325. The source for this quotation and those from other works by Plato (except for the quotation cited in footnote 4) is Benjamin Jowett, *The Dialogues of Plato*, 2 vols. (New York: Random House, 1937).
4. Plato *Republic* 401. The source for this quotation is Francis M. Cornford, *The Republic of Plato* (New York: Oxford University Press, 1945).
5. Plato *Protagoras* 325.

tions and praised for his answers, let him never rejoice in ignorance of anything . . . let him compete sometimes with others and quite often think himself victorious: let him also be excited by rewards, which at that age are eagerly sought after."[6] But since these positive techniques were to be utilized within the generally aversive context of the student being obliged to attend school, they do not alter the basic approach as being the overt provision of aversive effort-producing stimuli.

Exercise/Imitation Method: Explanation

Whereas the Telling/Showing Method requires minimum active involvement on the part of the student, the opposite is true of the Exercise/Imitation Method. The view of the learning process underlying this method is that the student must be relatively active in order to learn and that he must put forth considerable effort. Learning is assumed to increase gradually through practice. As in the case of the Telling/Showing Method, this method makes use of pre-response outcome-shaping stimuli and overtly provided, aversive effort-producing stimuli.

In the Exercise/Imitation Method the teacher may explicitly establish for the student the learning objective which he is to try to attain[7] or provide a model for the student to imitate, and/or stipulate the specific learning activities in which the student is to engage (without, however, expecting the student to gain an experience of "insight" from these activities).

A variety of techniques are appropriate to the Exercise/Imitation Method. Exercise would involve the use of drill, recitation, and different kinds of practice (such as practice in solving designated arithmetical problems). Imitation entails the setting of

6. Quintilian *Institutes of Oratory* 1. 1. 20. The source for this quotation and that cited in footnote 16 is William M. Smail, *Quintilian on Education* (New York: Teachers College Press, 1966).

7. The stipulation by the teacher of a goal to be attained presupposes that the student will on his own initiative undertake appropriate activities to achieve the goal. The teacher's purpose in specifying the goal when using the Exercise/Imitation Method is to be distinguished from the teacher's purpose in providing goal statements when the Telling/Showing Method is used. A teacher giving a lecture (the Telling/Showing Method), for example, may provide his students with an initial overview of what he plans to cover. In this latter case the purpose of the goal statement is to facilitate the learning of the specific information which is to follow—not to indicate to the student what he is expected to do.

objectives for the student to attain (for example, the assignment of a term paper) and the provision of various types of models which the student is required to emulate (for example, the imitation of penmanship models). The tasks assigned to the student when the Exercise/Imitation Method is employed may be verbal (as in memorization) or they may entail nonverbal experiences (as in the practice of physical skills).

Teachers who use the Exercise/Imitation Method usually assume that the activities required of the student will lead to fairly specific learning outcomes. For example, if a student completes the task of memorizing a list of fifty French verbs, he should then be able to respond correctly to questions concerning these fifty verbs. However, some teachers assume that the method may also produce a general improvement in the capability of the student, not just a specific improvement. In the example regarding the memorization of the fifty French verbs, adherents of the general improvement view (usually called the "mental discipline" view) would argue that the student during the act of memorizing the French verbs had also strengthened his general ability to memorize. They would contend that the improvement in the student's ability to memorize represents more than the acquisition of certain techniques of memorization; instead, they would say that practice in memorization actually increases the general retentiveness of the memory.

A frequently encountered instance of the mental discipline idea in contemporary educational practice is the justification that is given for including plane geometry in the high-school curriculum. It is admitted that plane geometry has little practical value for most students and that they will soon forget, for example, how to demonstrate that two triangles are congruent. But it is believed that the students will retain throughout their lives an improved ability to reason as a result of the mental exercises they performed in the plane-geometry class.

Exercise/Imitation Method: Documentation

An excellent brief statement on Exercise is found in Aristotle: "The virtues we get by first exercising them, as also happens in the case of the arts as well. For the things we have to learn before we can do them, we learn by doing them, e.g. men become builders by building and lyre players by playing the lyre."[8] Aristotle also recognized the fundamental importance of Imitation: "Imitation is natural to man from childhood, one of his advantages over the lower animals being this, that he is the most imitative creature in the world, and learns at first by imitation."[9]

The following two illustrations of the use of Exercise are among those contained in Plato's works. First: "Any one who could be good at anything must practice that thing from his youth upwards, both in sport and earnest, in its several branches: for example, he who is to be a good builder, should play at building children's houses; he who is to be a good husbandman, at tilling the ground; and those who have the care of their education should provide them when young with mimic tools."[10] Also: "In learning to write, the writing master first draws lines with a style for the use of the young beginner, and gives him the tablet and makes him follow the lines."[11] The use of Imitation in the training of an orator is described by Quintilian: "Let the young man . . . choose some orator, as was the custom among the ancients, whom he may follow and imitate."[12]

Several examples of the mental discipline idea may be cited from the classical writers on education. The following selection from Isocrates, in which the effects of certain studies are described as a "gymnastic of the mind," provides one of the clearest statements of mental discipline:

> Most men see in such studies [such as astronomy and geometry] nothing but empty talk and hair-splitting; for none of these disciplines has any useful application either to private or to public affairs; nay, they are not even remembered for any length of time after they are learned because

---

8. Aristotle *Nicomachean Ethics* 1103a, b. The source for all quotations from Aristotle is Richard McKeon, *The Basic Works of Aristotle* (New York: Random House, 1941).

9. Aristotle *Poetics* 1448b.

10. Plato *Laws* 643.

11. Plato *Protagoras* 326.

12. Quintilian *Institutes of Oratory* 10. 5. 19. The source for this quotation is John S. Watson, *Quintilian's Institutes of Oratory*, 2 vols. (London: George Bell and Sons, 1891).

they do not attend us through life nor do they lend aid in what we do, but are wholly divorced from our necessities. . . . [However,] while we are occupied with the subtlety and exactness of astronomy and geometry and are forced to apply our minds to difficult problems . . . we gain the power, after being exercised and sharpened on these disciplines, of grasping and learning more easily and more quickly those subjects which are of more importance and of greater value. . . . [Thus,] I would call it a gymnastic of the mind.[13]

Plato expressed a similar view of the benefits of arithmetic: "And have you further observed, that those who have a natural talent for calculation are generally quick at every other kind of knowledge; and even the dull, if they have had an arithmetical training, although they may derive no other advantage from it, always become much quicker than they would otherwise have been."[14]

The Exercise/Imitation Method lends itself to the utilization of games and play as instructional techniques. As well as providing outcome-shaping stimuli, games and play provide the student with an intrinsically pleasurable learning experience. But if the games and play take place within a compulsory education situation, then overall the teaching method would still have to be regarded as making use of overtly provided, aversive effort-producing stimuli. For example, if a student is obliged by his parents to attend school and if the teacher obliges him to participate in a game, then even if the game itself constitutes a pleasant experience the student is nevertheless aware that he will suffer unpleasant consquences if he refuses to cooperate.

Because it is not always appreciated that classical educational writers advocated making the learning experience enjoyable, two examples will be given. In the following excerpt, Plato describes the use of games in Egyptian schools: "In that country [Egypt] arithmetical games have been invented for the use of mere children, which they learn as a pleasure and amusement. They have to distribute apples and garlands, using the same number sometimes for a larger and sometimes for a lesser number of persons; and they

13. Isocrates *Antidosis* 261-267. The source for this quotation is *Isocrates,* vol. 2, trans. George Norlin (London: William Heinemann, 1929).
14. Plato *Republic* 526.

arrange [toy] pugilists and wrestlers as they pair together by lot or remain over, and show how their turns come in natural order."[15] The provision of pleasing instructional materials for students to play with is documented by Quintilian: "I approve of a practice devised to stimulate the child to learn, viz. that of giving him ivory letters to play with and anything else that can be proved to add to the child's pleasure, which it may be a delight to him to handle, look at, and name."[16]

Discovery/Restructuring Method: Explanation

The third traditional method of teaching we shall call the Discovery/Restructuring Method. It is similar to the other traditional methods in its reliance upon pre-response outcome-shaping stimuli and overtly provided, aversive effort-producing stimuli. Also, it is similar to the Exercise/Imitation Method in placing major reliance upon student activty to bring about the required learning outcome.

The feature which makes the Discovery/Restructuring Method different from the Exercise/Imitation Method is the expectation that the student will have an experience of insight in achieving the learning outcome. Thus, from the point of view of the student, the new learning is either *discovered,* or it is *restructured* out of what the student had learned previously.

It may sometimes be difficult to distinguish between the Exercise/Imitation Method and the Discovery/Restructuring Method, since both approaches entail activity on the part of the student. For example, both methods may involve a stipulation by the teacher of the specific learning activities that are required of the student. The only difference between the two methods in this example would be an expectation if the Discovery/Restructuring Method were being used that the student will experience a sense of insight, and the absence of such an expectation if the Exercise/ Imitation Method were being used.

15. Plato *Laws* 819.
16. Quintilian *Institutes of Oratory* 1. 1. 26.

To give another illustration of the difficulty of differentiating the two methods, a teacher using either of these two methods may know the specific learning outcomes he hopes to achieve. (In the case of the Exercise/Imitation Method, the teacher would always know what specific learning outcomes he hopes to achieve; in the case of Discovery/Restructuring, he may or may not.) If the teacher were using the Exercise/Imitation Method, he would be free to let the student know what the instructional goal is—as we previously indicated, informing the student about the learning objective he is expected to achieve is one of the procedures commonly employed with the Exercise/Imitation Method. However, if the teacher were using the Discovery/Restructuring Method, he could not tell the student what he is expected to learn, for if he were to do so, the student would not be in the position of "discovering" the learning outcome or "restructuring" previous learning in order to achieve a new insight.

Discovery/Restructuring Method: Documentation

The teaching techniques that are normally associated with the use of the Discovery/Restructuring Method include the technique of student-teacher discussions. Probably the best known example of the use of this technique during the Greco-Roman period is found in the so-called "Socratic Method." In this approach the teacher asks probing questions, first to bring the student to a realization that what he thought he knew previously he does not really know, and then to make the student discover "new" knowledge that somehow was already latent within him.[17]

17. It should be noted that the Socratic Method as practiced by Socrates did not actually make use of overtly provided, aversive effort-producing stimuli. Instead, Socrates's "students" came to him of their own free choice. Therefore, to be technically correct, we would have to classify Socrates's teaching procedure as an instance of a new teaching method that we will discuss in Chapter 3; but since Socrates did not explicitly recognize that his reliance on student-originated effort-producing stimuli represented a fundamentally different approach to teaching, we cannot credit him with the formulation of this new method. However, Socrates did seem to be aware that the use of outcome-shaping stimuli in his method was novel—hence his method serves as an excellent example of the use of outcome-shaping stimuli that is characteristic of the Discovery/Restructuring Method.

The following selection from Plato's dialogue *Meno* provides an excellent example of Socrates using his teaching method:

Socrates. And does he who desires the honourable also desire the good?

Meno. Certainly.

Soc. Then are there some who desire the evil and others who desire the good? Do not all men, my dear sir, desire good?

Men. I think not.

Soc. There are some who desire evil?

Men. Yes.

Soc. Do you mean that they think the evils which they desire, to be good; or do they know that they are evil and yet desire them?

Men. Both, I think.

Soc. And do you really imagine, Meno, that a man knows evils to be evils and desires them notwithstanding?

Men. Certainly I do.

Soc. And desire is of possession?

Men. Yes, of possession.

Soc. And does he think that the evils will do good to him who possesses them, or does he know that they will do him harm?

Men. There are some who think that the evils will do them good, and others who know that they will do them harm.

Soc. And, in your opinion, do those who think that they will do them good know that they are evils?

Men. Certainly not.

Soc. Is it not obvious that those who are ignorant of their nature do not desire them; but they desire what they suppose to be goods although they are really evils; and if they are mistaken and suppose the evils to be goods they really desire goods?

Men. Yes, in that case.

Soc. Well, and do those who, as you say, desire evils, and think that evils are hurtful to the possessor of them, know that they will be hurt by them?

Men. They must know it.

Soc. And must they not suppose that those who are hurt are miserable in proportion to the hurt which is inflicted upon them?

Men. How can it be otherwise?

Soc. But are not the miserable ill-fated?

Men. Yes, indeed.

Soc. And does any one desire to be miserable and ill-fated?

Men. I should say not, Socrates.

Soc. But if there is no one who desires to be miserable, there is no one, Meno, who desires evil; for what is misery but the desire and possession of evil?

Men. That appears to be the truth, Socrates, and I admit that nobody desires evil.

Soc. And yet, were you not saying just now that virtue is the desire and power of attaining good?

Men. Yes, I did say so.

Soc. But if this be affirmed, then the desire of good is common to all, and one man is no better than another in that respect?

Men. True.

Soc. And if one man is not better than another in desiring good, he must be better in the power of attaining it?

Men. Exactly.

Soc. Then, according to your definition, virtue would appear to be the power of attaining good?

Men. I entirely approve, Socrates, of the manner in which you now view this matter.

Soc. Then let us see whether what you say is true from another point of view; for very likely you may be right: —You affirm virtue to be the power of attaining goods?

Men. Yes.

Soc. And the goods which you mean are such as health and wealth and the possession of gold and silver, and having office and honour in the state—those are what you would call goods?

Men. Yes, I should include all those.

Soc. Then, according to Meno, who is the hereditary friend of the great king, virtue is the power of getting silver and gold; and would you add that they must be gained piously, justly, or do you deem this to be of no consequence? And is any mode of acquisition, even if unjust and dishonest, equally to be deemed virtue?

Men. Not virtue, Socrates, but vice.

Soc. Then justice or temperance or holiness, or some other part of virtue, as would appear, must accompany the acquisition, and without them the mere acquisition of good will not be virtue.

Men. Why, how can there be a virtue without these?

Soc. And the non-acquisition of gold and silver in a dishonest manner for oneself or another, or in other words the want of them, may be equally virtue?

Men. True.

Soc. Then the acquisition of such goods is no more virtue than the non-acquisition and want of them, but whatever is accompanied by justice or honesty is virtue, and whatever is devoid of justice is vice.

Men. It cannot be otherwise, in my judgment.

Soc. And were we not saying just now that justice, temperance, and the like, were each of them a part of virtue?

Men. Yes.

Soc. And so, Meno, this is the way in which you mock me.

Men. Why do you say that, Socrates?

Soc. Why, because I asked you to deliver virtue into my hands whole and unbroken, and I gave you a pattern according to which you were to frame your answer; and you have forgotten already, and tell me that virtue is the power of attaining good justly, or with justice; and justice you acknowledge to be a part of virtue.

Men. Yes.

Soc. Then it follows from your own admissions, that virtue is doing what you do with a part of virtue; for justice and the like are said by you to be parts of virtue.

Men. What of that?

Soc. What of that! Why, did not I ask you to tell me the nature of virtue as a whole? And you are very far from telling me this; but declare every action to be virtue which is done with a part of virtue; as though you had told me and I must already know the whole of virtue, and this too when frittered away into little pieces. And therefore, my dear Meno, I fear that I must begin again and repeat the same question: What is virtue? For otherwise, I can only say, that every action done with a part of virtue is virtue; what else is the meaning of saying that every action done with justice is virtue? Ought I not to ask the question over again; for can any one who does not know virtue know a part of virtue?

Men.   No; I do not say that he can.

Soc.   Do you remember how, in the example of figure, we rejected any answer given in terms which were as yet unexplained or unadmitted?

Men.   Yes, Socrates; and we were quite right in doing so.

Soc.   But then, my friend, do not suppose that we can explain to any one the nature of virtue as a whole through some unexplained portion of virtue, or anything at all in that fashion; we should only have to ask over again the old question, What is virtue? Am I not right?

Men.   I believe that you are.

Soc.   Then begin again, and answer me, What, according to you and your friend Gorgias, is the definition of virtue?

Men.   O Socrates, I used to be told, before I knew you, that you were always doubting yourself and making others doubt; and now you are casting your spells over me, and I am simply getting bewitched and enchanted, and am at my wits' end. And if I may venture to make a jest upon you, you seem to me both in your appearance and in your power over others to be very like the flat torpedo fish, who torpifies those who come near him and touch him, as you have now torpified me, I think. For my soul and my tongue are really torpid, and I do not know how to answer you; and though I have been delivered of an infinite variety of speeches about virtue before now, and to many persons—and very good ones they were, as I thought—at this moment I cannot even say what virtue is. And I think that you are very wise in not voyaging and going away from home, for if you did in other places as you do in Athens, you would be cast into prison as a magician.[18]

Plan for the Forthcoming Chapters

We have now obtained a partial answer to the question we raised at the beginning of this chapter: "How many fundamentally different methods of teaching have been devised, and what are the

18. Plato *Meno* 77-80.

characteristics of the basic teaching methods?" We have found that the Greek and Roman writers on education were acquainted with three different basic teaching methods, which we have labeled the Telling/Showing Method, the Exercise/Imitation Method, and the Discovery/Restructuring Method.

In the chapters which follow we shall attempt to examine the views of several of the important Western educational writers who lived since the Greco-Roman period. We shall begin our survey with an analysis of the ideas of John Amos Comenius in the next chapter. Since Comenius was born in 1592, this means that we are neglecting an interval of about fifteen hundred years. Although many distinguished educational writers made their contributions during this omitted period—such as St. Augustine (354-430), Alcuin (735-804), Peter Abelard (1079-1142), and Juan Luis Vives (1492-1540)—none of these writers formulated a new basic teaching method. Even Comenius, as we shall see, did not develop any new teaching methods. But we have chosen to deal with Comenius in the next chapter because many historians of education consider that his writings constitute the starting point from which modern views of teaching method have emerged. Our selection of modern writers is a subjective one, but we have attempted to include all of the authors who have been generally credited with providing significant statements on teaching method.

Selected Bibliography

General Works

BROUDY, HARRY S., and PALMER, JOHN R. *Exemplars of Teaching Method*. Chicago: Rand McNally, 1965.

BRUMBAUGH, ROBERT S., and LAWRENCE, NATHANIEL M. *Philosophers on Education: Six Essays on the Foundations of Western Thought*. Boston: Houghton Mifflin, 1963.

COLMAN, JOHN E. *The Master Teachers and the Art of Teaching*. New York: Pitman, 1967.

CURTIS, S. J., and BOULTWOOD, M. E. A. *A Short History of Educational Ideas*. 3rd ed. London: University Tutorial Press, 1961.

DUPUIS, ADRIAN M. *Philosophy of Education in Historical Perspective*. Chicago: Rand McNally, 1966.

FRANKENA, WILLIAM K. *Three Historical Philosophies of Education: Aristotle, Kant, and Dewey.* Glenview, Ill.: Scott, Foresman, 1965.

GAGE, N. L., ed. *Handbook of Research on Teaching.* New York: Macmillan, 1963.

GAGE, N. L. "Teaching Methods." In *Encyclopedia of Educational Research,* edited by Robert L. Ebel. 4th ed. New York: Macmillan, 1969.

HARDIE, CHARLES D. *Truth and Fallacy in Educational Theory.* New York: Teachers College Press, 1962.

HILGARD, ERNEST R., ed. *Theories of Learning and Instruction.* Sixty-third Yearbook of the NSSE, Part I. Chicago: National Society for the Study of Education, 1964.

HYMAN, RONALD T., ed. *Contemporary Thought on Teaching.* Englewood Cliffs, N. J.: Prentice-Hall, 1971.

HYMAN, RONALD T. *Ways of Teaching.* Philadelphia: J. B. Lippincott, 1970.

JOYCE, BRUCE, AND WEIL, MARSHA. *Models of Teaching.* Englewood Cliffs, N. J.: Prentice-Hall, 1972.

MOSSTON, MUSKA. *Teaching: From Command to Discovery.* Belmont, Calif.: Wadsworth, 1972.

POWER, EDWARD J. *Evolution of Educational Doctrine: Major Educational Theorists of the Western World.* New York: Appleton-Century-Crofts, 1969.

QUICK, ROBERT H. *Essays on Educational Reformers.* New York: Appleton, 1896.

RUSK, ROBERT R. *The Doctrines of the Great Educators.* Rev. ed. London: Macmillan, 1955.

SAETTLER, PAUL. *A History of Instructional Technology.* New York: McGraw-Hill, 1968.

SIEGEL, LAURENCE, ed. *Instruction: Some Contemporary Viewpoints.* San Francisco: Chandler, 1967.

SKINNER, B. F. *The Technology of Teaching.* New York: Appleton-Century-Crofts, 1968.

WALTON, JOHN. *Toward Better Teaching in the Secondary Schools.* Boston: Allyn and Bacon, 1966.

Traditional Teaching Methods

BECK, FREDERICK A. G. *Greek Education: 450-350 B.C.* London: Methuen, 1964.

BURNET, JOHN, ed. *Aristotle on Education.* Cambridge: Cambridge University Press, 1967.

CLARK, DONALD L. *Rhetoric in Greco-Roman Education.* New York: Columbia University Press, 1957.

JOHNSON, MAURITZ. "Who Discovered Discovery?" *Phi Delta Kappan* 48 (1966): 120-23.

KENNEDY, GEORGE. *Quintilian.* New York: Twayne, 1969.

KOLESNIK, WALTER B. *Mental Discipline in Modern Education.* Madison: University of Wisconsin Press, 1962.

LODGE, R. C. *Plato's Theory of Education.* London: Routledge and Kegan Paul, 1947.

MARROU, H. I. *A History of Education in Antiquity.* Translated by George Lamb. New York: Mentor, 1964.

MONROE, PAUL. *Source Book of the History of Education for the Greek and Roman Period.* New York: Macmillan, 1932.

NETTLESHIP, RICHARD L. *The Theory of Education in the Republic of Plato.* London: Oxford University Press, 1939.

NORLIN, GEORGE. *Isocrates.* Cambridge, Mass.: Harvard University Press, 1966.

SMAIL, WILLIAM M. *Quintilian on Education.* New York: Teachers College Press, 1966.

WOODY, THOMAS. *Life and Education in Early Societies.* New York: Macmillan, 1949.

2

John Amos Comenius

Although several important statements on education were produced after the Greco-Roman period and prior to 1600, it is John Amos Comenius (1592-1670) who is generally regarded as the "father of modern education."[1] Nicholas Murray Butler, the well-known president of Columbia University, asserted that Comenius occupies a place in education that is "of commanding importance. He introduces and dominates the whole modern movement in the field of elementary and secondary education. His relation to our present teaching is similar to that held by Copernicus and Newton toward modern science, and Bacon and Descartes toward modern philosophy."[2] A similar judgment about the importance of Comenius is expressed by his biographer and translator M. W. Keatinge: "There are few problems in education that are not discussed by him, and teachers cannot fail to derive stimulus from a perusal of the answers that this great schoolmaster . . . gave to the questions that are still being asked at the present day."[3]

1. Ernest M. Eller, ed., *The School of Infancy by John Amos Comenius* (Chapel Hill: University of North Carolina Press, 1956), p. 17.
2. Nicholas Murray Butler, *The Meaning of Education: Contributions to a Philosophy of Education,* rev. ed. (New York: Scribner's, 1915), pp. 295-96.
3. M. W. Keatinge, *Comenius* (New York: McGraw-Hill, 1931), p. 15.

Comenius was born March 28, 1592, in the village of Nivnitz, which is now in Czechoslovakia. After studying at the University of Heidelberg, Comenius became a priest for the Moravian Brethren in 1616; in 1632 he was consecrated as a bishop. In addition to his episcopal duties, Comenius wrote extensively on religious and educational topics. The most outstanding work by Comenius on education is *The Great Didactic*. This book was written first in Czech between 1628 and 1632, and then composed in Latin as the *Didactica magna* in 1636 (the Latin edition was first published in 1657, the Czech version in 1849, while the first English translation appeared in 1896). Comenius died in Amsterdam, November 15, 1670.

Comenius was interested in discovering a natural method of teaching. In the following selection from *The Great Didactic* Comenius expresses his belief in the possibility of an effective teaching method, which he thinks can be derived from an imitation of nature.

The duty of the teachers of the young . . . is none other than to skilfully scatter the seeds of instruction in their minds, and to carefully water God's plants. . . .

Is there any who denies that sowing and planting need skill and experience? If an unpractised gardener plant an orchard with young trees, the greater number of them die, and the few that prosper do so rather through chance than through skill. But the trained gardener goes to work carefully, since he is well instructed, where, when, and how to act and what to leave alone, that he may meet with no failure. . . .

Hitherto the method of instruction has been so uncertain that scarcely any one would dare to say: "In so many years I will bring this youth to such and such a point. I will educate him in such and such a way." We must therefore see if it be possible to place the art of intellectual discipline on such a firm basis that sure and certain progress may be made. . . .

I maintain that a method can be found by means of which each person will be enabled to bring into his mental consciousiness not only what he has learned, but more as well; since he will recall with ease all that he has learned from teachers or from books, and, at the same time, will be able to pass sound judgment on the objective facts to which his information refers. . . .

As soon as we have succeeded in finding the proper method it will be no harder to teach school-boys, in any number desired, than with the help of the printing-press to cover a thousand sheets daily with the neatest writing, or with Archimedes' machine to move houses, towers, and immense weights, or to cross the ocean in a ship, and journey to the New World. The whole process, too, will be as free from friction as is the movement of a clock whose motive power is supplied by the weights. It will be as pleasant to see education carried out on my plan as to look at an automatic machine of this kind, and the process will be as free from failure as are these mechanical contrivances, when skillfully made. . . .

Let us then commence to seek out, in God's name, the principles on which, as on an immovable rock, the method of teaching and of learning can be grounded. If we wish to to find a remedy for the defects of nature, it is in nature herself that we must look for it, since it is certain that art can do nothing unless it imitate nature. . . .

It is now quite clear that that order, which is the dominating principle in the art of teaching all things to all men, should be, and can be, borrowed from no other source but the operations of nature. As soon as this principle is thoroughly secured, the processes of art will proceed as easily and as spontaneously as those of nature. Very aptly does Cicero say: "If we take nature as our guide, she will never lead us astray," and also: "Under the guidance of nature it is impossible to go astray." This is our belief, and our advice is to watch the operations of nature carefully and to imitate them.[4]

Comenius did not, as we shall see, originate a method of teaching that is different from any of those which had been em-

---

4. M. W. Keatinge, *The Great Didactic of John Amos Comenius* (London: Adam and Charles Black, 1896), pp. 263, 263-64, 264, 294-95, 248-49, 250, 252. Reprinted with permission.

The following system will be used throughout this book for page references to quoted material: page numbers given in the footnote identify sequentially each segment of text that is separated by a final punctuation mark and an ellipsis. Extraneous numberings, headings, and internal footnotes have usually been eliminated from the quotations.

ployed in ancient Greece and Rome. But he did stress that the outcome-shaping stimuli should consist of nonverbal experiences.
Comenius's views on the use of outcome-shaping stimuli are presented in the following three selections. These views correspond
respectively with the use of outcome-shaping stimuli in each of
the three traditional teaching methods: Telling/Showing, Exer-
cise/Imitation, and Discovery/Restructuring.

Those things, therefore, that are placed before
the intelligence of the young, must be real things and not the
shadows of things. I repeat, they must be *things*; and by the
term I mean determinate, real, and useful things that can
make an impression on the senses and on the imagination.
But they can only make this impression when brought sufficiently near.

From this a golden rule for teachers may be derived.
Everything should, as far as is possible, be placed before
the senses. Everything visible should be brought before the
organ of sight, everything audible before that of hearing.
Odours should be placed before the sense of smell, and
things that are tastable and tangible before the sense of taste
and of touch respectively. If an object can make an impression on several senses at once, it should be brought into contact with several. . . .

Since the senses are the most trusty servants of the
memory, this method of sensuous perception, if universally
applied, will lead to the permanent retention of knowledge
that has once been acquired. For instance, if I have once
tasted sugar, seen a camel, heard a nightingale sing, or been
in Rome, and have on each occasion attentively impressed
the fact on my memory, the incidents will remain fresh and
permanent. We find, accordingly, that children can easily
learn Scriptural and secular stories from pictures. Indeed, he
who has once seen a rhinoceros (even in a picture) or been
present at a certain occurrence, can picture the animal to
himself and retain the event in his memory with greater ease
than if they had been described to him six hundred times.
Hence the saying of Plautus: "An eye-witness is worth more
than ten ear-witnesses." Horace also says: "What is entrusted
to the fickle ears makes less impression on the mind than
things which are actually presented to the eyes and which
the spectator stores up for himself."

In the same manner, whoever has once seen a dissection of the human body will understand and remember the relative position of its parts with far greater certainty than if he had read the most exhaustive treatises on anatomy, but had never actually seen a dissection performed. Hence the saying, "Seeing is believing."

If the objects themselves cannot be procured, representations of them may be used. Copies or models may be constructed for teaching purposes, and the same principle may be adopted by botanists, geometricians, zoologists, and geographers, who should illustrate their descriptions by engravings of the objects described. The same thing should be done in books on physics and elsewhere. For example, the human body will be well explained by ocular demonstration if the following plan be adopted. A skeleton should be procured (either such an one as is usually kept in universities, or one made of wood), and on this framework should be placed the muscles, sinews, nerves, veins, arteries, as well as the intestines, the lungs, the heart, the diaphragm, and the liver. These should be made of leather and stuffed with wool, and should be of the right size and in the right place, while on each organ should be written its name and its function. If you take the student of medicine to this construction and explain each part to him separately, he will grasp all the details without any effort, and from that time forth will understand the mechanism of his own body. For every branch of knowledge similar constructions (that is to say, images of things which cannot be procured in the original) should be made, and should be kept in the schools ready for use. It is true that expense and labour will be necessary to produce these models, but the result will amply reward the effort.[5]

*   *   *   *   *

What has to be done must be learned by practice. Artisans do not detain their apprentices with theories, but set them to do practical work at an early stage; thus they learn to forge by forging, to carve by carving, to paint by painting, and to dance by dancing. In schools, therefore, let the students learn to write by writing, to talk by talking, to sing by singing, and to reason by reasoning. In this way

5. *Ibid.*, pp. 336-37, 337-39. Emphasis in the original.

schools will become work-shops humming with work, and
students whose efforts prove successful will experience the
truth of the proverb: "We give form to ourselves and to our
materials at the same time."

A definite model of that which has to be made must
always be provided.

This the student should first examine, and then imitate,
as though he were following in the footsteps of a guide. For
he who neither knows what has to be done nor how to do it,
is unable to produce anything of himself, but must have a
model placed before him. Indeed it is sheer cruelty to force
any one to do what you wish, while he is ignorant what your
wishes are; to demand, that is to say, that he form straight
lines, right angles, or perfect circles, unless you first give him
a ruler, a square, and a pair of compasses, and explain their
use to him. Further, great care should be taken to provide in
the school-room formulæ for or models of everything that
has to be made, and these, whether drawings and diagrams,
or rules and models, should be correct, definite, and simple;
easy both to understand and to imitate. There will then be
no absurdity in demanding of a man that he see, when provided with a light; that he walk, when he already stands on
his feet; or that he use the tools that are already in his hands.

The use of instruments should be shown in practice
and not by words; that is to say, by example rather than by
precept.

It is many years since Quintilian said: "Through precepts the way is long and difficult, while through examples
it is short and practicable." But alas, how little heed the
ordinary schools pay to this advice. The very beginners in
grammar are so overwhelmed by precepts, rules, exceptions
to the rules, and exceptions to the exceptions, that for the
most part they do not know what they are doing, and are
quite stupefied before they begin to understand anything.
Mechanics do not begin by drumming rules into their apprentices. They take them into the workshop and bid them
look at the work that has been produced, and then, when
they wish to imitate this (for man is an imitative animal),
they place tools in their hands and show them how they
should be held and used. Then, if they make mistakes, they
give them advice and correct them, often more by example
than by mere words, and, as the facts show, the novices

easily succeed in their imitation. For there is great truth in that saying of the Germans, "A good leader finds a good follower." Very apposite, too, is the remark of Terence, "Do you go before; I will follow." This is the way, namely, by imitating, and without any laborious rules, that children learn to walk, to run, to talk, and to play. Rules are like thorns to the understanding, and to grasp their meaning needs both attention and ability, while even the dullest students are aided by example. No one has ever mastered any language or art by precept alone; while by practice this is possible, even without precept.[6]

* * * * *

The proper education of the young does not consist in stuffing their heads with a mass of words, sentences, and ideas dragged together out of various authors, but in opening their understanding to the outer world, so that a living stream may flow from their own minds, just as leaves, flowers, and fruit spring from the buds on a tree, while in the following year a fresh bud is again formed and a fresh shoot, with its leaves, flowers, and fruit, grows from it.

Hitherto the schools have not taught their pupils to develope their minds like young trees from their own roots, but rather to deck themselves with branches plucked from other trees, and, like Æsop's crow, to adorn themselves with the feathers of other birds; they have taken no trouble to open the fountain of knowledge that is hidden in the scholars, but instead have watered them with water from other sources. That is to say, they have not shown them the objective world as it exists in itself, but only what this, that, or the other author has written or thought about this or that object, so that he is considered the most learned who best knows the contradictory opinions which many men have held about many things. The result is that most men possess no information but the quotations, sentences, and opinions that they have collected by rummaging about in various authors, and thus piece their knowledge together like a patchwork quilt. "Oh you imitators, you slavish pack!" cries Horace. A slavish pack indeed, and accustomed to carry burdens that are not their own.

6. *Ibid.*, pp. 347-48.

But why, I ask you, do we allow ourselves to be led astray by the opinions of other men, when what is sought is a knowledge of the true nature of things? Have we nothing better to do than to follow others to their cross-roads and down their by-ways, and to study attentively the deviation that each makes from the right path? O brother mortals! let us hasten to the goal and give up this idle wandering. If our goal be firmly set before us, why should we not hasten to it by the shortest road; why should we use the eyes of other men in preference to our own?

The methods by which all branches of knowledge are taught show that it really is the schools that are to blame for this; that they really teach us to see by means of the eyes of others, and to become wise by employing their brains. For these methods do not teach us to discover. . . .

We arrive therefore at the following conclusion: men must, as far as possible, be taught to become wise by studying the heavens, the earth, oaks, and beeches, but not by studying books; that is to say, they must learn to know and investigate the things themselves, and not the observations that other people have made about the things.[7]

Our next selection constitutes a typical example of the style of presentation in *The Great Didactic*. Proceeding from the description of a natural phenomenon, Comenius indicates how man generally imitates this phenomenon, next shows how school practices have deviated from nature, and finally states what must be done to rectify the deviation.

Nature Does Not Hurry, But Advances Slowly

For example, a bird does not place its eggs in the fire, in order to hatch them quickly, but lets them develope slowly under the influence of natural warmth. Neither, later on, does it cram its chickens with food that they may mature quickly (for this would only choke them), but it selects their food with care and gives it to them gradually in the quantities that their weak digestion can support.

Imitation. The builder, too, does not erect the walls on the foundations with undue haste and then straightway put on the roof; since, unless the foundations were given

7. *Ibid.*, pp. 299-300; 302.

time to dry and become firm, they would sink under the superincumbent weight, and the whole building would tumble down. Large stone buildings, therefore, cannot be finished within one year, but must have a suitable length of time allotted for their construction.

Nor does the gardener expect a plant to grow large in the first month, or to bear fruit at the end of the first year. He does not, therefore, tend and water it every day, nor does he warm it with fire or with quicklime, but is content with the moisture that comes from heaven and with the warmth that the sun provides.

Deviation. For the young, therefore, it is torture
(i) If they are compelled to receive six, seven, or eight hours' class instruction daily, and private lessons in addition.

(ii) If they are overburdened with dictations, with exercises, and with the lessons that they have to commit to memory, until nausea and, in some cases, insanity is produced.

If we take a jar with a narrow mouth (for to this we may compare a boy's intellect) and attempt to pour a quantity of water into it violently, instead of allowing it to trickle in dry by drop, what will be the result? Without doubt the greater part of the liquid will flow over the side, and ultimately the jar will contain less than if the operation had taken place gradually. Quite as foolish is the action of those who try to teach their pupils, not as much as they can assimilate, but as much as they themselves wish; for the faculties need to be supported and not to be overburdened, and the teacher, like the physician, is the servant and not the master of nature.

Rectification. The ease and pleasantness of study will therefore be increased:
(i) If the class instruction be curtailed as much as possible, namely to four hours, and if the same length of time be left for private study.

(ii) If the pupils be forced to memorise as little as possible, that is to say, only the most important things; of the rest they need only grasp the general meaning.

(iii) If everything be arranged to suit the capacity of the pupil, which increases naturally with study and age.[8]

8. *Ibid.*, pp. 288-89.

As the first excerpt below shows, Comenius was concerned with the necessity for motivating students to participate in the teaching-learning process and advocated the use of overtly provided, aversive effort-producing techniques. We may conclude, therefore, that Comenius's views of teaching method meet the criteria of the three traditional methods of instruction. Despite his comprehensiveness, his engaging writing style, and the contemporary tone of many of his ideas, he did not succeed in formulating a new basic teaching method.

But there are passages in *The Great Didactic* which express a different point of view about the use of effort-producing stimuli, as exemplified in our final excerpt. In this selection Comenius appears to reject the use of overtly provided, aversive effort-producing stimuli; he suggests that students will learn most effectively if education is made a pleasant experience and they are permitted to learn according to their own interests. As we shall see in Chapter 3, this notion anticipates the achievement of Jean Jacques Rousseau in developing a new teaching method.

There is a proverb in Bohemia, "A school without discipline is like a mill without water," and this is very true. For, if you withdraw the water from a mill, it stops, and, in the same way, if you deprive a school of discipline, you take away from it its motive power. A field also, if it be never ploughed, produces nothing but weeds; and trees, if not continually pruned, revert to their wild state and bear no fruit. It must not be thought, however, that we wish our schools to resound with shrieks and with blows. What we demand is vigilance and attention on the part of the master and of the pupils. For discipline is nothing but an unfailing method by which we may make our scholars, scholars in reality. . . .

The master should try to keep his pupils up to their work.

(1) He should give them frequent examples of the conduct that they should try to imitate, and should point to himself as a living example. Unless he does this, all his work will be in vain.

(2) He may employ advice, exhortation, and sometimes blame, but should take great care to make his motive

clear and to show unmistakably that his actions are based
on paternal affection, and are destined to build up the characters of his pupils and not to crush them. Unless the pupil
understands this and is fully persuaded of it, he will despise
all discipline and will deliberately resist it.

(3) Finally, if some characters are unaffected by gentle methods, recourse must be had to more violent ones, and
every means should be tried before any pupil is pronounced
impossible to teach. Without doubt there are many to whom
the proverb, "Beating is the only thing that improves a
Phrygian," applies with great force. And it is certain that,
even if such measures do not produce any great effect on
the boy who is punished, they act as a great stimulus to the
others by inspiring them with fear. We should take great
care, however, not to use these extreme measures too read-
ily, or too zealously, as, if we do, we may exhaust all our
resources before the extreme case of insubordination which
they were intended to meet, arises.[9]

*　*　*　*　*

Truly did Aristotle say that all men are born
anxious to acquire knowledge. . . . In practice, however, the
tender indulgence of parents hinders the natural tendency
of children, and later on frivolous society leads them into
idle ways, while the various occupations of city and court
life, and the external circumstances which surround them,
turn them away from their real inclinations. Thus it comes
to pass that they show no desire to investigate what is unknown, and cannot concentrate their thoughts with ease.
(For just as the tongue, when permeated with one flavour,
judges another with difficulty, so the mind, when occupied
with one subject, finds it hard to give its attention to another). In these cases the external distraction must first be
removed; nature will then assert itself with its original
vigour, and the desire for knowledge will once more be ap-
parent. But how many of those who undertake to educate
the young appreciate the necessity of first teaching them
how to acquire knowledge? The turner shapes a block of
wood with his axe before he turns it; the blacksmith heats
iron before he hammers it; the clothweaver, before he spins

9. *Ibid.*, pp. 401, 404.

his wool, first cleans, washes, cards, and fulls it; the shoe-maker, before he sews the shoe, prepares, shapes, and smooths the leather; but who, I ask, ever thinks it necessary that the teacher, in the same way, should make his pupils anxious for information, capable of receiving instruction, and therefore ready for a many-sided education, before he begins to place knowledge before them? Teachers almost in-variably take their pupils as they find them; they turn them, beat them, card them, comb them, drill them into certain forms, and expect them to become a finished and polished product; and if the result does not come up to their expec-tation (and I ask you how could it?) they are indignant, angry, and furious. And yet we are surprised that some men shrink and recoil from such a system. Far more is it matter for surprise that any one can endure it at all. . . .

Therefore

(i) The desire to know and to learn should be excited in boys in every possible manner.

(ii) The method of instruction should lighten the drud-gery of learning, that there may be nothing to hinder the scholars or deter them from making progress with their studies.

The desire to learn is kindled in boys by parents, by masters, by the school, by the subjects of instruction, by the method of teaching, and by the authority of the state.

By parents, if they praise learning and the learned in the presence of their children, or if they encourage them to be industrious by promising them nice books and clothes, or some other pretty thing; if they commend the teachers (espe-cially him to whom they entrust their sons) as much for their friendly feeling towards the pupils as for their skill in teach-ing (for love and admiration are the feelings most calculated to stimulate a desire for imitation); finally, if, from time to time, they send the child to him with a small present. In this way they will easily bring it about that the children like their lessons and their teachers, and have confidence in them.

By the teachers, if they are gentle and persuasive, and do not alienate their pupils from them by roughness, but attract them by fatherly sentiments and words; if they com-mend the studies that they take in hand on account of their excellence, pleasantness, and ease; if they praise the indus-trious ones from time to time (to the little ones they may give apples, nuts, sugar, etc.); if they call the children to them, privately or in the class, and show them pictures of the things that they must learn, or explain to them optical or geometrical instruments, astronomical globes, and such-like things that are calculated to excite their admiration; or again, if they occasionally give the children some message to carry to their parents. In a word, if they treat their pupils kindly they will easily win their affections, and will bring it about that they prefer going to school to remaining at home.

The school itself should be a pleasant place, and attractive to the eye both within and without. Within, the room should be bright and clean, and its walls should be ornamented by pictures. These should be either portraits of celebrated men, geographical maps, historical plans, or other ornaments. Without, there should be an open place to walk and to play in (for this is absolutely necessary for children, as we shall show later), and there should also be a garden attached, into which the scholars may be allowed to go from time to time and where they may feast their eyes on trees, flowers, and plants. If this be done, boys will, in all probability, go to school with as much pleasure as to fairs, where they always hope to see and hear something new.

The subjects of instruction themselves prove attractive to the young, if they are suited to the age of the pupil and are clearly explained; especially if the explanation be relieved by a humorous or at any rate by a less serious tone. For thus the pleasant is combined with the useful.

If the method is to excite a taste for knowledge, it must, in the first place, be natural. For what is natural takes place without compulsion. Water need not be forced to run down a mountain-side. If the dam, or whatever else holds it back, be removed, it flows down at once. It is not necessary to persuade a bird to fly; it does so as soon as the cage is opened. The eye and the ear need no urging to enjoy a fine painting or a beautiful melody that is presented to them. In all these cases it is more often necessary to restrain than to urge on. . . .

In the second place, if the scholars are to be interested, care must be taken to make the method palatable, so that everything, no matter how serious, may be placed before them in a familiar and attractive manner; in the form of a dialogue, for instance, by pitting the boys against one another to answer and explain riddling questions, comparisons, and fables. . . .

The civil authorities and the managers of schools can kindle the zeal of the scholars by being present at public performances (such as declarations, disputations, examinations, and promotions), and by praising the industrious ones and giving them small presents (without respect of person).[10]

Selected Bibliography

DOBINSON, C. H., ed. *Comenius and Contemporary Education.* Hamburg: Unesco Institute for Education, 1970.

MONROE, WILL S. *Comenius and the Beginnings of Educational Reform.* New York: Scribner's, 1900.

NEEDHAM, JOSEPH, ed. *The Teacher of Nations.* Cambridge: Cambridge University Press, 1942.

SADLER, JOHN E. *J. A. Comenius and the Concept of Universal Education.* New York: Barnes and Noble, 1966.

SPINKA, MATTHEW. *John Amos Comenius: That Incredible Moravian.* Chicago: University of Chicago Press, 1943.

10. *Ibid.*, pp. 239, 239-40, 282-84, 284, 284.

3

Jean Jacques Rousseau

Jean Jacques Rousseau must be accorded a unique place among Western educational writers, for he is the only one who can be credited with both the formulation and elaboration of a fundamentally different conception of instructional method. Rousseau's ideas on the new method are contained in his book *Emile*. The new method, which we shall call the Student Interest Method, differs from the three traditional methods in that it substitutes student-originated effort-producing stimuli for overtly provided, aversive effort-producing stimuli.

In its other characteristics the Student Interest Method encompasses the three traditional methods. For example, a self-motivated student might ask a teacher for a verbal explanation (which would be identical in terms of the use of outcome-shaping stimuli to the Telling/Showing Method), he might ask the teacher to give him a model to imitate (which would make this part of the procedure comparable to the Exercise/Imitation Method), or he might engage in a discussion with the teacher (which, if the teacher tried to bring about an experience of insight, would be equivalent to the use of outcome-shaping stimuli in the Discovery/Restructuring Method).

Thus, in the Student Interest Method, the essential requirement is for the student to be interested in something and, as a result of this interest, to seek to learn. But in the real world there are probably few children who are not exposed to aversive parental inducements to study or who are not subject to compulsory education laws. Therefore, we need to distinguish between two forms of the Student Interest Method: the *extended* form and the *restricted* form. In the extended form, aversive teacher and societal direction of effort-producing stimuli is absent. In the restricted form, aversive society-directed effort-producing stimuli may be present, but within the classroom the teacher makes it clear to the student that he is not required to learn anything. If he wants to play or to relax, he is freely permitted to do so. Although the teacher may indirectly try to secure student effort by structuring his environment (for example, by providing various centers of interest in the classroom), there is no aversive teacher direction of the effort-producing stimuli in order to bring about student participation in the teaching-learning process. The student would always have the option of withdrawing from the learning situation at any time if he should so desire.

Rousseau is also known as one of the world's outstanding political philosophers. He was born in Geneva, June 28, 1712, and went to Paris in 1742. His two greatest writings, *The Social Contact* and *Emile,* were published in the same year (1762). But he was persecuted for his ideas and was compelled to flee to Switzerland and later to England. Returning to France in 1767, he died at Ermenonville on July 2, 1778.

Our first selection from *Emile* provides an explanation of why Rousseau thinks a new approach to teaching method that emphasizes the desires of the child is necessary.

Although we know approximately the limits of human life and our chances of attaining those limits, nothing is more uncertain than the length of the life of any one of us. Very few reach old age. The chief risks occur at the beginning of life; the shorter our past life, the less we must hope to live. Of all the children who are born scarcely one half reach adolescence, and it is very likely your pupil will not live to be a man.

What is to be thought, therefore, of that cruel education which sacrifices the present to an uncertain future, that burdens a child with all sorts of restrictions and begins by making him miserable, in order to prepare him for some far-off happiness which he may never enjoy? Even if I considered that education wise in its aims, how could I view without indignation those poor wretches subjected to an intolerable slavery and condemned like galley-slaves to endless toil, with no certainty that they will gain anything by it? The age of harmless mirth is spent in tears, punishments, threats, and slavery. You torment the poor thing for his good; you fail to see that you are calling Death to snatch him from these gloomy surroundings. Who can say how many children fall victims to the excessive care of their fathers and mothers? They are happy to escape from this cruelty; this is all that they gain from the ills they are forced to endure: they die without regretting, having known nothing of life but its sorrows.

Men, be kind to your fellow-men; this is your first duty, kind to every age and station, kind to all that is not foreign to humanity. What wisdom can you find that is greater than kindness? Love childhood, indulge its sports, its pleasures, its delightful instincts. Who has not sometimes regretted that age when laughter was ever on the lips, and when the heart was ever at peace? Why rob these innocents of the joys which pass so quickly, of that precious gift which they cannot abuse? Why fill with bitterness the fleeting days of early childhood, days which will no more return for them than for you? Fathers, can you tell when death will call your children to him? Do not lay up sorrow for yourselves by robbing them of the short span which nature has allotted to them. As soon as they are aware of the joy of life, let them rejoice in it, so that whenever God calls them they may not die without having tasted the joy of life.

How people will cry out against me! I hear from afar the shouts of that false wisdom which is ever dragging us onwards, counting the present as nothing, and pursuing without a pause a future which flies as we pursue, that false wisdom which removes us from our place and never brings us to any other.

Now is the time, you say, to correct his evil tendencies; we must increase suffering in childhood, when it is less keenly felt, to lessen it in manhood. But how do you know that you can carry out all these fine schemes; how do you know that all this fine teaching with which you overwhelm the feeble mind of the child will not do him more harm than good in the future? How do you know that you can spare him by anything by the vexations you heap upon him now? Why inflict on him more ills than befit his present condition unless you are quite sure that these present ills will save him future ill? And what proof can you give me that those evil tendencies you profess to cure are not the result of your foolish precautions rather than of nature? What a poor sort of foresight, to make a child wretched in the present with the more or less doubtful hope of making him happy at some future day. If such blundering thinkers fail to distinguish between liberty and licence, between a merry child and a spoilt darling, let them learn to discriminate.

Let us not forget what befits our present state in the pursuit of vain fancies. Mankind has its place in the sequence of things; childhood has its place in the sequence of human life; the man must be treated as a man and the child as a child. Give each his place, and keep him there.[1]

Rousseau's concern in *Emile* is to depict the education that he would like to provide for an imaginary young boy who has the name Emile. The boy is to be taught by a tutor (who is represented in the book as being Rousseau himself) in a country setting remote from the influence of the city. The following selection from *Emile* provides a very explicit statement of the notion that the student must be interested if he is to learn.

When I . . . get rid of children's lessons, I get rid of the chief cause of their sorrows, namely their books. Reading is the curse of childhood, yet it is almost the only occupation you can find for children. Emile, at twelve years old, will hardly know what a book is. "But," you say, "he must, at least, know how to read." When reading is of use to him, I admit he must learn to read, but till then he will only find it a nuisance.

1. Jean Jacques Rousseau, *Emile*, trans. Barbara Foxley (New York: E. P. Dutton, 1911), pp. 42-44. Reprinted with permission.

If children are not to be required to do anything as a matter of obedience, it follows that they will only learn what they perceive to be of real and present value, either for use or enjoyment; what other motive could they have for learning? The art of speaking to our absent friends, of hearing their words; the art of letting them know at first hand our feelings, our desires, and our longings, is an art whose usefulness can be made plain at any age. How is it that this art, so useful and pleasant in itself, has become a terror to children? Because the child is compelled to acquire it against his will, and to use it for purposes beyond his comprehension. A child has no great wish to perfect himself in the use of an instrument of torture, but make it a means to his pleasure, and soon you will not be able to keep him from it.

People make a great fuss about discovering the best way to teach children to read. They invent "bureaux"[2] and cards, they turn the nursery into a printer's shop. Locke would have them taught to read by means of dice. What a fine idea! And the pity of it! There is a better way than any of those, and one which is generally overlooked—it consists in the desire to learn. Arouse this desire in your scholar and have done with your "bureaux" and your dice—any method will serve.

Present interest, that is the motive power, the only motive power that takes us far and safely. Sometimes Emile receives notes of invitation from his father or mother, his relations or friends; he is invited to a dinner, a walk, a boating expedition, to see some public entertainment. These notes are short, clear, plain, and well written. Some one must read them to him, and he cannot always find anybody when wanted; no more consideration is shown to him than he himself showed to you yesterday. Time passes, the chance is lost. The note is read to him at last, but it is too late. Oh! if only he had known how to read! He receives other notes, so short, so interesting, he would like to try to read them. Sometimes he gets help, sometimes none. He does his best, and at last he makes out half the note; it is something about going tomorrow to drink cream—Where? With whom? He cannot

2. *Translator's note.* The "bureau" was a sort of case containing letters to be put together to form words. It was a favourite device for the teaching of reading and gave its name to a special method, called the bureau-method, of learning to read.

tell—how hard he tries to make out the rest! I do not think Emile will need a "bureau." Shall I proceed to the teaching of writing? No, I am ashamed to toy with these trifles in a treatise on education.

I will just add a few words which contain a principle of great importance. It is this—What we are in no hurry to get is usually obtained with speed and certainty. I am pretty sure Emile will learn to read and write before he is ten, just because I care very little whether he can do so before he is fifteen; but I would rather he never learnt to read at all, than that this art should be acquired at the price of all that makes reading useful. What is the use of reading to him if he always hates it? . . .

The more I urge my method of letting well alone, the more objections I perceive against it. If your pupil learns nothing from you, he will learn from others. If you do not instil truth he will learn falsehoods; the prejudices you fear to teach him he will acquire from those about him, they will find their way through every one of his senses; they will either corrupt his reason before it is fully developed or his mind will become torpid through inaction, and will become engrossed in material things. If we do not form the habit of thinking as children, we shall lose the power of thinking for the rest of our life.

I fancy I could easily answer that objection, but why should I answer every objection? If my method itself answers your objections, it is good; if not, it is good for nothing. I continue my explanation.

If, in accordance with the plan I have sketched, you follow rules which are just the opposite of the established practice, if instead of taking your scholar far afield, instead of wandering with him in distant places, in far-off lands, in remote centuries, in the ends of the earth, and in the very heavens themselves, you try to keep him to himself, to his own concerns, you will then find him able to perceive, to remember, and even to reason; this is nature's order. As the sentient being becomes active his discernment develops along with his strength. Not till his strength is in excess of what is needed for self-preservation, is the speculative faculty developed, the faculty adapted for using this superfluous strength for other purposes. Would you cultivate your pupil's intelligence, cultivate the strength it is meant to control.

Give his body constant exercise, make it strong and healthy, in order to make him good and wise; let him work, let him do things, let him run and shout, let him be always on the go; make a man of him in strength, and he will soon be a man in reason.

Of course by this method you will make him stupid if you are always giving him directions, always saying come here, go there, stop, do this, don't do that. If your head always guides his hands, his own mind will become useless. But remember the conditions we laid down; if you are a mere pedant it is not worth your while to read my book.[3]

The teacher who uses the Student Interest Method does not give up his control of the teaching-learning process—if he did so he could not be called a teacher. But the teacher must rely on indirect or positive control rather than overtly aversive control to secure the initial involvement of the student in the instructional process, as Rousseau explains in the following excerpt.

Young teacher, I am setting before you a difficult task, the art of controlling without precepts, and doing everything without doing anything at all. This art is, I confess, beyond your years, it is not calculated to display your talents nor to make your value known to your scholar's parents; but it is the only road to success. You will never succeed in making wise men if you do not first make little imps of mischief. This was the education of the Spartans; they were not taught to stick to their books, they were set to steal their dinners. Were they any the worse for it in after life? Ever ready for victory, they crushed their foes in every kind of warfare, and the prating Athenians were as much afraid of their words as of their blows.

When education is most carefully attended to, the teacher issues his orders and thinks himself master, but it is the child who is really master. He uses the tasks you set him to obtain what he wants from you, and he can always make you pay for an hour's industry by a week's complaisance. You must always be making bargains with him. These bargains, suggested in your fashion, but carried out in his, always follow the direction of his own fancies, especially when

3. Rousseau, *Emile*, pp. 80-82, 82.

you are foolish enough to make the condition some advantage he is almost sure to obtain, whether he fulfils his part of the bargain or not. The child is usually much quicker to read the master's thoughts than the master to read the child's feelings. And that is as it should be, for all the sagacity which the child would have devoted to self-preservation, had he been left to himself, is now devoted to the rescue of his native freedom from the chains of his tyrant; while the latter, who has no such pressing need to understand the child, sometimes finds that it pays him better to leave him in idleness or vanity.

Take the opposite course with your pupil; let him always think he is master while you are really master. There is no subjection so complete as that which preserves the forms of freedom; it is thus that the will itself is taken captive. Is not this poor child, without knowledge, strength, or wisdom, entirely at your mercy? Are you not master of his whole environment so far as it affects him? Cannot you make of him what you please? His work and play, his pleasure and pain, are they not, unknown to him, under your control? No doubt he ought only to do what he wants, but he ought to want to do nothing but what you want him to do. He should never take a step you have not foreseen, nor utter a word you could not foretell.

Then he can devote himself to the bodily exercises adapted to his age without brutalising his mind; instead of devloping his cunning to evade an unwelcome control, you will then find him entirely occupied in getting the best he can out of his environment with a view to his present welfare, and you will be surprised by the subtlety of the means he devises to get for himself such things as he can obtain, and to really enjoy things without the aid of other people's ideas. You leave him master of his own wishes, but you do not multiply his caprices. When he only does what he wants, he will soon only do what he ought, and although his body is constantly in motion, so far as his sensible and present interests are concerned, you will find him developing all the reason of which he is capable, far better and in a manner much better fitted for him than in purely theoretical studies.

Thus when he does not find you continually thwarting him, when he no longer distrusts you, no longer has anything to conceal from you, he will neither tell you lies nor deceive you; he will show himself fearlessly as he really is, and you can study him at your ease, and surround him with all the lessons you would have him learn, without awaking his suspicions.

Neither will he keep a curious and jealous eye on your own conduct, nor take a secret delight in catching you at fault. It is a great thing to avoid this. One of the child's first objects is, as I have said, to find the weak spots in its rulers. Though this leads to spitefulness, it does not arise from it, but from the desire to evade a disagreeable control. Over-burdened by the yoke laid upon him, he tries to shake it off, and the faults he finds in his master give him a good opportunity for this. Still the habit of spying out faults and delighting in them grows upon people. Clearly we have stopped another of the springs of vice in Emile's heart. Having nothing to gain from my faults, he will not be on the watch for them, nor will he be tempted to look out for the faults of others.

All these methods seem difficult because they are new to us, but they ought not to be really difficult. I have a right to assume that you have the knowledge required for the business you have chosen; that you know the usual course of development of the human thought, that you can study mankind and man, that you know beforehand the effect on your pupil's will of the various objects suited to his age which you put before him. You have the tools and the art to use them; are you not master of your trade?[4]

Since often the child may not derive intrinsic satisfaction from the activity of learning, indirect control by the teacher means starting with a known interest of the child and then structuring a situation so that the child is required to learn in order to satisfy his interest. Rousseau describes this procedure in the following excerpt (which pertains to another boy, not Emile). In this example the boy would like to have a cake, and the teacher wants him to learn how to run. Without overtly coercing the child, the teacher uses the child's interest in the cake as the means for inducing him to run.

An idle, lazy child was to be taught to run. He had no liking for this or any other exercise, though he was

4. *Ibid.*, pp. 84-85.

intended for the army. Somehow or other he had got it into his head that a man of his rank need know nothing and do nothing—that his birth would serve as a substitute for arms and legs, as well as for every kind of virtue. The skill of Chiron himself would have failed to make a fleet-footed Achilles of this young gentleman. The difficulty was increased by my determination to give him no kind of orders. I had renounced all right to direct him by preaching, promises, threats, emulation, or the desire to show off. How should I make him want to run without saying anything? I might run myself, but he might not follow my example, and this plan had other drawbacks. Moreover, I must find some means of teaching him through this exercise, so as to train mind and body to work together. This is how I, or rather how the teacher who supplied me with this illustration, set about it.

When I took him a walk of an afternoon I sometimes put in my pocket a couple of cakes, of a kind he was very fond of; we each ate one while we were out, and we came back well pleased with our outing. One day he noticed I had three cakes; he could have easily eaten six, so he ate his cake quickly and asked for the other. "No," said I, "I could eat it myself, or we might divide it, but I would rather see those two little boys run a race for it." I called them to us, showed them the cake, and suggested that they should race for it. They were delighted. The cake was placed on a large stone which was to be the goal; the course was marked out, we sat down, and at a given signal off flew the children! The victor seized the cake and ate it without pity in the sight of the spectators and of his defeated rival.

The sport was better than the cake; but the lesson did not take effect all at once, and produced no result. I was not discouraged, nor did I hurry; teaching is a trade at which one must be able to lose time and save it. Our walks were continued, sometimes we took three cakes, sometimes four, and from time to time there were one or two cakes for the racers. If the prize was not great, neither was the ambition of the competitors. The winner was praised and petted, and everything was done with much ceremony. To give room to run and to add interest to the race I marked out a longer course and admitted several fresh competitors. Scarcely had they entered the lists than all the passers-by stopped to watch. They were encouraged by shouting, cheering, and clapping. I sometimes saw my little man trembling with excitement, jumping up and shouting when one was about to reach or overtake another—to him these were the Olympian games.

However, the competitors did not always play fair, they got in each other's way, or knocked one another down, or put stones on the track. That led us to separate them and make them start from different places at equal distances from the goal. You will soon see the reason for this, for I must describe this important affair at length.

Tired of seeing his favourite cakes devoured before his eyes, the young lord began to suspect that there was some use in being a quick runner, and seeing that he had two legs of his own, he began to practise running on the quiet. I took care to see nothing, but I knew my stratagem had taken effect. When he thought he was good enough (and I thought so too), he pretended to tease me to give him the other cake. I refused; he persisted, and at last he said angrily, "Well, put it on the stone and mark out the course, and we shall see." "Very good," said I, laughing, "You will get a good appetite, but you will not get the cake." Stung by my mockery, he took heart, won the prize, all the more easily because I had marked out a very short course and taken care that the best runner was out of the way. It will be evident that, after the first step, I had no difficulty in keeping him in training. Soon he took such a fancy for this form of exercise that without any favour he was almost certain to beat the little peasant boys at running, however long the course.[5]

In the first of our last two selections Rousseau enunciates the principle "never substitute the symbol for the thing," which is reminiscent of Comenius's preference for the use of nonverbal experiences in teaching. The second selection reiterates this point and goes on to provide a specific example of the Student Interest Method. Rousseau describes how Emile's interest in returning home may be utilized as the means of inducing him to learn how to find his way. (Except for the element of student interest to replace aversive teacher and/or society-directed effort-producing

5. *Ibid.*, pp. 105-107.

stimuli, the teaching procedure in this example would be the same as that of the Discovery/Restructuring Method).

Man's diverse powers are stirred by the same instinct. The bodily activity, which seeks an outlet for its energies, is succeeded by the mental activity which seeks for knowledge. Children are first restless, then curious; and this curiosity, rightly directed, is the means of development for the age with which we are dealing. Always distinguish between natural and acquired tendencies. There is a zeal for learning which has no other foundation than a wish to appear learned, and there is another which springs from man's natural curiosity about all things far or near which may affect himself. The innate desire for comfort and the impossibility of its complete satisfaction impel him to the endless search for fresh means of contributing to its satisfaction. This is the first principle of curiosity; a principle natural to the human heart, though its growth is proportional to the development of our feeling and knowledge. If a man of science were left on a desert island with his books and instruments and knowing that he must spend the rest of his life there, he would scarcely trouble himself about the solar system, the laws of attraction, or the differential calculus. He might never even open a book again; but he would never rest till he had explored the furthest corner of his island, however large it might be. Let us therefore omit from our early studies such knowledge as has no natural attraction for us, and confine ourselves to such things as instinct impels us to study.

Our island is this earth; and the most striking object we behold is the sun. As soon as we pass beyond our immediate surroundings, one or both of these must meet our eye. Thus the philosophy of most savage races is mainly directed to imaginary divisions of the earth or to the divinity of the sun.

What a sudden change you will say. Just now we were concerned with what touches ourselves, with our immediate environment, and all at once we are exploring the round world and leaping to the bounds of the universe. This change is the result of our growing strength and of the natural bent of the mind. While we were weak and feeble, self-preservation concentrated our attention on ourselves; now that we are strong and powerful, the desire for a wider sphere carries us beyond ourselves as far as our eyes can reach. But as the intellectual world is still unknown to us, our thoughts are bounded by the visible horizon, and our understanding only develops within the limits of our vision.

Let us transform our sensations into ideas, but do not let us jump all at once from the objects of sense to objects of thought. The latter are attained by means of the former. Let the senses be the only guide for the first workings of reason. No book but the world, no teaching but that of fact. The child who reads ceases to think, he only reads. He is acquiring words not knowledge.

Teach your scholar to observe the phenomena of nature; you will soon rouse his curiosity, but if you would have it grow, do not be in too great a hurry to satisfy this curiosity. Put the problems before him and let him solve them himself. Let him know nothing because you have told him, but because he has learnt it for himself. Let him not be taught science, let him discover it. If ever you substitute authority for reason he will cease to reason; he will be a mere plaything of other peoples' thoughts.

You wish to teach this child geography and you provide him with globes, spheres, and maps. What elaborate preparations! What is the use of all these symbols; why not begin by showing him the real thing so that he may at least know what you are talking about?

One fine evening we are walking in a suitable place where the wide horizon gives us a full view of the setting sun, and we note the objects which mark the place where it sets. Next morning we return to the same place for a breath of fresh air before sun-rise. We see the rays of light which announce the sun's approach; the glow increases, the east seems afire, and long before the sun appears the light leads us to expect its return. Every moment you expect to see it. There it is at last! A shining point appears like a flash of lightning and soon fills the whole space; the veil of darkness rolls away, man perceives his dwelling place in fresh beauty. During the night the grass has assumed a fresher green; in the light of early dawn, and gilded by the first rays of the sun, it seems covered with a shining network of dew reflecting the light and colour. The birds raise their chorus of praise to greet the Father of life, not one of them is mute; their gentle warbling is softer than by day, it expresses the langour of a peaceful waking. All these produce an impression of freshness which seems to reach the very soul. It is a brief hour of enchantment which no man can resist; a sight so grand, so fair, so delicious, that none can behold it unmoved.

Fired with this enthusiasm, the master wishes to impart it to the child. He expects to rouse his emotion by drawing attention to his own. Mere folly! The splendour of nature lives in man's heart; to be seen, it must be felt. The child sees the objects themselves, but does not perceive their relations, and cannot hear their harmony. It needs knowledge he has not yet acquired, feelings he has not yet experienced, to receive the complex impression which results from all these separate sensations. If he has not wandered over arid plains, if his feet have not been scorched by the burning sands of the desert, if he has not breathed the hot and oppressive air reflected from the glowing rocks, how shall he delight in the fresh air of a fine morning. The scent of flowers, the beauty of foliage, the moistness of the dew, the soft turf beneath his feet, how shall all these delight his senses. How shall the song of the birds arouse voluptuous emotion if love and pleasure are still unknown to him? How shall he behold with rapture the birth of this fair day, if his imagination cannot paint the joys it may bring in its track? How can he feel the beauty of nature, while the hand that formed it is unknown?

Never tell the child what he cannot understand: no descriptions, no eloquence, no figures of speech, no poetry.[6]

✻   ✻   ✻   ✻   ✻

I do not like verbal explanations. Young people pay little heed to them, nor do they remember them. Things! Things! I cannot repeat it too often. We lay too much stress upon words; we teachers babble, and our scholars follow our example.

Suppose we are studying the course of the sun and the way to find our bearings, when all at once Emile interrupts me with the question, "What is the use of that?" what a fine lecture I might give, how many things I might take occasion to teach him in reply to his question, especially if there is any one there. I might speak of the advantages of travel, the

6. *Ibid.*, pp. 130-32.

value of commerce, the special products of different lands and the peculiar customs of different nations, the use of the calendar, the way to reckon the seasons for agriculture, the art of navigation, how to steer our course at sea, how to find our way without knowing exactly where we are. Politics, natural history, astronomy, even morals and international law are involved in my explanation, so as to give my pupil some idea of all these sciences and a great wish to learn them. When I have finished I shall have shown myself a regular pedant, I shall have made a great display of learning, and not one single idea has he understood. He is longing to ask me again, "What is the use of taking one's bearings?" but he dare not for fear of vexing me. He finds it pays best to pretend to listen to what he is forced to hear. This is the practical result of our fine systems of education.

But Emile is educated in a simpler fashion. We take so much pains to teach him a difficult idea that he will have heard nothing of all this. At the first word he does not understand, he will run away, he will prance about the room, and leave me to speechify by myself. Let us seek a more commonplace explanation; my scientific learning is of no use to him.

We were observing the position of the forest to the north of Montmorency when he interrupted me with the usual question, "What is the use of that?" "You are right," I said. "Let us take time to think it over, and if we find it is no use we will drop it, for we only want useful games." We find something else to do and geography is put aside for the day.

Next morning I suggest a walk before breakfast; there is nothing he would like better; children are always ready to run about, and he is a good walker. We climb up to the forest, we wander through its clearings and lose ourselves; we have no idea where we are, and when we want to retrace our steps we cannot find the way. Time passes, we are hot and hungry; hurrying vainly this way and that we find nothing but woods, quarries, plains, not a landmark to guide us. Very hot, very tired, very hungry, we only get further astray. At last we sit down to rest and to consider our position. I assume that Emile has been educated like an ordinary child. He does not think, he begins to cry; he has no idea we are close to Montmorency, which is hidden from our view by a mere thicket; but this thicket is a forest to him, a man of his size is buried among bushes. After a few minutes' silence I begin anxiously—

Jean Jacques. My dear Emile, what shall we do to get out?

Emile. I am sure I do not know. I am tired, I am hungry, I am thirsty. I cannot go any further.

Jean Jacques. Do you suppose I am any better off? I would cry too if I could make my breakfast off tears. Crying is no use, we must look about us. Let us see your watch; what time is it?

Emile. It is noon and I am so hungry!

Jean Jacques. Just so; it is noon and I am so hungry too.

Emile. You must be very hungry indeed.

Jean Jacques. Unluckily my dinner won't come to find me. It is twelve o'clock. This time yesterday we were observing the position of the forest from Montmorency. If only we could see the position of Montmorency from the forest—

Emile. But yesterday we could see the forest, and here we cannot see the town.

Jean Jacques. That is just it. If we could only find it without seeing it.

Emile. Oh! my dear friend!

Jean Jacques. Did not we say the forest was—

Emile. North of Montmorency.

Jean Jacques. Then Montmorency must lie—

Emile. South of the forest.

Jean Jacques. We know how to find the north at midday.

Emile. Yes, by the direction of the shadows.

Jean Jacques. But the south?

Emile. What shall we do?

Jean Jacques. The south is opposite the north.

Emile. That is true; we need only find the opposite of the shadows. That is the south! That is the south! Montmorency must be over there! Let us look for it there!

Jean Jacques. Perhaps you are right; let us follow this path through the wood.

Emile. (*Clapping his hands.*) Oh, I can see Montmorency! there it is, quite plain, just in front of us! Come to luncheon, come to dinner, make haste! Astronomy is some use after all.

Be sure that he thinks this if he does not say it; no matter which, provided I do not say it myself. He will certainly never forget this days' lesson as long as he lives, while if I had only led him to think of all this at home, my lecture would have been forgotten the next day. Teach by doing whenever you can, and only fall back upon words when doing is out of the question.[7]

Selected Bibliography

BOYD, WILLIAM. *The Educational Theory of Jean Jacques Rousseau.* London: Longmans, Green, 1911.

BOYD, WILLIAM, ed. *The Minor Writings of Jean Jacques Rousseau.* New York: Bureau of Publications, Teachers College, Columbia University, 1962.

BROOME, JACK H. *Rousseau: A Study of His Thought.* New York: Barnes and Noble, 1963.

DOBINSON, C. H. *Jean-Jacques Rousseau.* London: Methuen, 1969.

GUÉHENNO, JEAN. *Jean-Jacques Rousseau.* Translated by John and Doreen Weightman. 2 vols. New York: Columbia University Press, 1966.

7. *Ibid.*, pp. 143-44.

4

Johann Heinrich Pestalozzi

Some historians of education have expressed a very high opinion of Johann Heinrich Pestalozzi. Robert Ulich, for example, has declared that "Pestalozzi's example of 'Let the little children come unto me' probably had a greater effect on modern education than all that philosophers ever said or wrote about the tasks and character of education."[1] On the other hand, Robert Rusk has stated that "among the great educators Pestalozzi cuts a sorry figure; he appears a man afflicted with new ideas which he found himself unable to formulate or to put effectively into practice."[2]

Pestalozzi was born in Zurich, Switzerland, on January 12, 1746. He attended the Collegium Humanitatis and the Collegium Carolinum in Zurich, but gave up the idea of a career in the Church or law to become a farmer in 1769 at Neuhof. He provided a school for poor children on his farm for about five years, but was forced to abandon this effort. Pestalozzi resumed his teaching career in 1798 when he took charge of an orphanage in Stanz. During 1799-1804, as a schoolmaster at Burgdorf, he experimented with new teaching techniques and attracted considerable attention;

1. Robert Ulich, *History of Educational Thought* (New York: American Book Company, 1945), p. 264.
2. Robert R. Rusk, *The Doctrines of the Great Educators,* rev. ed. (London: Macmillan, 1955), p. 186.

during this period he also produced two basic works on instructional method: "The Method" in 1800 and *How Gertrude Teaches Her Children* in 1801. From 1805 to 1825 he conducted a school in Yverdon, which was internationally famous as a place where his teaching techniques were demonstrated. Pestalozzi died at Brugg on February 17, 1827.

Many educational historians have suggested that Pestalozzi's view of instructional method is based on that of Jean Jacques Rousseau, and that his principal contribution to teaching method was to show how Rousseau's ideas could be applied in the classroom. "Historical commonplace makes Rousseau the theorist and lets Pestalozzi, following the trail blazed by Rousseau, invent natural methods for teachers."[3] Pestalozzi did, in fact, attempt to raise his own son (whom he named Jean Jacques and referred to by the diminutive Jacobli) in accordance with what he considered to be the method described in *Emile*. But, as the following excerpt from Pestalozzi's diary indicates, he resorted to aversive teacher direction of the effort-producing stimuli rather than rely on student origination.

> **January 27th, 1774.** I called his [Jacobli's] attention to some running water. He was delighted, and, as I walked on down the hill, followed me, saying to the water: "Wait a moment; I shall be back directly." Presently I took him to the side of the same stream again. "Look," he cried, "the water comes down too; it runs from up there and goes lower and lower." As we followed the course of the stream, I repeated several times: "Water flows down hill."
>
> I told him the names of a few animals, saying: "The dog, the cat, etc., are animals, but your uncle, John, Nicholas, are men." I then asked him: "What is a cow, a sheep, the minister, a goat, your cousin, etc?" and he answered correctly nearly every time, his wrong answers being accompanied by a sort of smile which seemed to say that he did not mean to answer properly. I think behind this fun there must be a desire to see how far his will is independent of mine?

3. Edward J. Power, *Evolution of Educational Doctrine: Major Educational Theorists of the Western World* (New York: Appleton-Century-Crofts, 1969), p. 275.

January 29th. I succeeded in making him sit for a long time at his lessons, after having first made him run and play out of doors in the cold. I can see that a man must be robust himself if he is to concern himself with his pupil's open-air games.

January 30th. He was soon tired of learning to read, but as I had decided that he should work at it regularly every day, whether he liked it or not, I determined to make him feel the necessity of doing so, from the very first, by showing him there was no choice between this work and my displeasure, which I made him feel by keeping him in. It was only after having been punished in this way three times that he at last conquered his impatience. From that time he did his work willingly and cheerfully. . . .

[**February 2nd.**] I could only get him to read with difficulty; he has a thousand ways of getting out of it, and never loses an opportunity of doing something else. When he wants something he cannot get, he very cleverly pretends that what he wants would help him in his lessons, or in his reading. I have been much struck by these tricks for some days past; it is clearly my duty to watch them with the greatest care.

February 3rd. I felt again to-day, no less strongly than yesterday, what a vicious system ours is for teaching a child to count. All words learned without thinking produce almost hopeless confusion in our minds, but how clear our knowledge would be, if we could receive the truth without alloy! O God! who art my Father and the Father of my child, teach me to understand the holy natural laws by which Thou preparest us slowly by means of an innumerable variety of impressions for conceiving exact and complete ideas, of which words are but the signs.

When the child knows the signs before learning to know the things they represent, and especially when he connects false ideas with them, our daily lessons and conversation do but fortify and increase his error and push him the further along a wrong path without our even suspecting it. How difficult it then is to correct the evil, whereas, by proceeding slowly from truth to truth, we should be following the luminous path of Nature.

February 4th. Since yesterday Jacobli has not been well. To-day feverish symptoms frightened us, and we sent for the doctor. We had much difficulty to get the child to take any medicine. The doctor suggested that we should occasionally make him drink something unpleasant, but harmless, when quite well, in order that he might get so accustomed to it that when really ill he would no longer mind it. At first sight this seems to me a good idea, and I should be inclined to extend it to apply to education generally.

February 13th. Our care of Jacobli during his illness has made him more self-willed. I took a nut from him to crack it; he thought I was going to eat it and yelled with anger. I looked at him coldly, and then, without a word, took a second nut and ate them both before his eyes. He did not stop crying; I held him a looking-glass; he rushed off to hide himself.

I have often admired the simple wisdom of our servant Nicholas. In the matter of education I am usually very anxious to learn the ideas of people who have been brought up quite naturally and without restraint, who have been taught by life itself and not by lessons. "Nicholas," I said, "don't you think Jacobli has a good memory?" "Yes, he said; "but you overload it." This was just what I had often been afraid of. "But," I said, "if the child were overburdened, I think we should notice it; he would lose heart and become timid and restless, at the very first symptoms of which I should of course stop." "Ah," said Nicholas, "then you really are anxious about the boy's spirit and happiness? That is just what I was afraid you would overlook." Right, Nicholas! No education would be worth a jot that resulted in a loss of of manliness and lightness of heart. So long as there is joy in the child's face, ardour and enthusiasm in all his games, so long as happiness accompanies most of his impressions, there is nothing to fear. Short moments of self-subjugation quickly followed by new interests and new joys do not dishearten. . . .

February 15th. I have noticed to-day that my child has a habit which shows his cleverness, but which I must watch most carefully. When he asks for anything, he always begins either by answering objections which he thinks likely to be made, or by giving reasons why the request should be granted. "Mamma, I won't break it; I only want to look at it; I will use it in my lessons; I only want one." We must take care that this trick does not succeed. An open, straightforward request is what we should like. When he asks in this roundabout way, we ought to insist on his making his request again in a simple manner. It would perhaps be well to refuse what he does not ask for properly.

Lead your child out into Nature, teach him on the hilltops and in the valleys. There he will listen better, and the sense of freedom will give him more strength to overcome difficulties. But in these hours of freedom let him be taught by Nature rather than by you. Let him fully realize that she is the real teacher and that you, with your art, do nothing more than walk quietly at her side. Should a bird sing or an insect hum on a leaf, at once stop your talk; bird and insect are teaching him; you may be silent.

But in those few hours of study devoted to the steady acquirement of necessary knowledge, you must suffer no interruption. Let such hours be few, but let them be inviolable. The least irregularity in this respect must be immediately corrected. Make it impossible for the child to have the faintest hope of being able to escape this duty. Such a hope would encourage restlessness, where as the certainty that there is no escape will cause even the desire to escape to be forgotten. In this case, indeed, Nature must no longer be listened to, and the child's desire for freedom must be resisted.

A father who guides wisely and blames justly must be obeyed by his child, but no unnecessary command must be given. Never let your orders be the result of caprice, or vanity, or a partiality for knowledge which is not essential. To ensure obedience it is most important that children should know exactly what is forbidden. Nothing produces so much bitter feeling as the punishment of ignorance as a fault. If you punish an innocent child you lose your hold on his heart. We must not imagine that a child knows by instinct what is harmful and what things are held to be important.

Plenty of joy and liberty, with a few periods of restraint, during which the child has to fight against and subdue his natural desires, will give strength and the power of endurance. Too much restraint would have a disheartening effect, and joys coming more rarely would no longer have the same happy influence. The character is formed by the strongest and most frequent impressions, all others are comparatively powerless. That is why it is possible for education to correct defects, and why the maxim is no less false than discouraging which says that a few chance impressions suffice to undo the work of the most careful educator.

Jacobli has been self-willed and violent; I have been obliged to punish him several times to-day.

February 16th and 17th. To cure his stubbornness and avoid the daily renewal of the same rebukes, which, unfortunately, is beginning to be necessary, I must be more careful to alternate his lessons with his games, and not curtail his liberty unnecessarily; I must also decide definitely exactly how much time is to be set apart for actual study, so that nothing he learns at other times may seem like work.

I have taught him to hold his pencil. Although this is a very small matter, I will never let him hold it badly again. . . .

February 19th. I find myself sometimes embarrassed through having given up, with all other pedantries, the master's tone of authority. Where shall I draw the line between liberty and obedience, that social life so soon compels us to draw?

Reasons for Liberty

It is impossible to curtail a child's liberty without, to some extent, incurring his dislike.

Experience proves that children who have been too much under restraint, make up for it later by excesses in the opposite direction.

Restraint excites various passions.

A wise liberty induces the child to keep his eyes and ears open, and makes him contented, happy, and even-tempered.

But this complete liberty supposes a preliminary education, which has taught the child submission to the nature of things, though not to the will of man.

Reasons for Obedience

Without it there is no education possible. There are crises, indeed, when the child would be ruined by being

allowed his liberty. Even under the most favourable circumstances it is impossible not to thwart his will occasionally.

Liberty does not stifle the passions, it only delays their
development. It is vanity, for instance, that makes Emile
tremble in his desire to excel the juggler. And does not
Rousseau himself recognize the state of dependence in which
society places us, when he says that there are some men of
such passionate natures that they would certainly have to
be subjected to restraint in their youth, if their childhood
had been left entirely free.

Social life demands such talents and habits as it is not
possible to form without restraining the child's liberty.

Which of these is the true position and which the false?
Liberty is good, and so is obedience. We must reconcile
what Rousseau separated when, struck by the evils of the
unwise restraint that only tends to degrade humanity, he
advocated unbounded liberty.

Let us endeavour to see how far he was right, and
profit by his wisdom.

I would say to the teacher: Be thoroughly convinced of
the immense value of liberty; do not let vanity make you
anxious to see your efforts producing premature fruit; let
your child be as free as possible, and seek diligently for
every means of ensuring his liberty, peace of mind, and good
humour. Teach him absolutely nothing by words that you
can teach him by the things themselves; let him see for himself, hear, find out, fall, pick himself up, make mistakes; no
word, in short, when action is possible. What he can do for
himself, let him do it; let him be always occcupied, always
active, and let the time you leave him to himself represent
by far the greatest part of his childhood. You will then see
that Nature teaches him better than men.

But when you see the necessity of accustoming him to
obedience, prepare yourself with the greatest care for this
duty, the most difficult of all in such an education as we are
considering. Remember that if restraint robs you of your
pupil's confidence, all your labour is lost. Make sure, then,
of his heart, and let him feel that you are necessary to him.
Be merrier and pleasanter than any of his companions; in
his games let him prefer you to all the rest.

He must trust you. If he often asks for something you
do not think good, tell him what the consequences will be,

and leave him his liberty. But you must take care that the consequences are such as he will not easily forget. Always show him the right way. Should he leave it and fall into the mire, go to his rescue, but do not shield him from the unpleasant results of having enjoyed complete liberty, and of not having listened to your warnings. In this way his trust in you will be so great that it will not be shaken even when you have to thwart him. He must obey the wise teacher or the father he has learned to respect; but only in cases of necessity must an order be given.[4]

In the following excerpt from *How Gertrude Teaches Her Children*, Pestalozzi describes his first experiences as a schoolmaster in Stanz. As far as effort-producing stimuli are concerned, he seems to rely upon aversive teacher direction. The outcome-shaping stimuli are pre-response and involve considerable student activity. At times he assumes that gradual student learning through practice will result; at other times he seems to suggest that discovery may take place.

In addition to giving an account of Pestalozzi's ideas on teaching method, this excerpt also exemplifies a difficulty that is encountered many times in the analysis of the writings of the great educators. This difficulty is that the writer may think he is describing a single teaching method, but a careful analysis according to the criteria of our classification system reveals that he uses more than one assumption about how learning takes place. Our ascription of a particular teaching method or methods to a given writer, therefore, simply reflects our judgment as to what was the predominant conception of teaching method held by the writer; it does not mean that indications of other methods cannot also be found in his writings.

I went [to Stanz to work in a school.] I would have gone to the hindmost cavern of the mountains to come nearer my end [of becoming a schoolmaster,] and now I really did come nearer it; but imagine my position—I alone —deprived of all the means of education; I alone, overseer, paymaster, handy man, and almost servant maid, in an un-

4. Roger De Guimps, *Pestalozzi: His Life and Work* (New York: Appleton, 1895), pp. 40-41, 42-43, 44-46, 46-48.

finished house, surrounded by ignorance, disease, and novelty of all kinds. The number of children increased gradually to eighty, all of different ages; some full of pretensions, others wayside beggars; all, except a few, wholly ignorant. What a task! to form and develop these children! What a task!

I dared to attempt it, and stood in their midst pronouncing sounds, and making them imitate them.

Whoever saw it was astonished at the result. It was like a meteor that is seen in the air, and vanishes again. No one knew its nature. I understood it not myself. It was the result of a simple psychological idea which I felt but of which I was not clearly aware. . . .

So I worked in Stanz until the approach of the Austrians took the heart out of my work, and the feelings that now oppressed me brought my physical powers to the state in which they were when I left Stanz.

Up to this point I was not yet certain of the foundations of my procedure. But as I was attempting the impossible, I found that possible which I had not expected; and as I pushed through the pathless thicket that no one had trodden for ages, I found footprints in it leading to the high road, which for ages had been untrodden.

I will go a little into details. As I was obliged to give the children instruction, alone, and without help, I learned the art of teaching many together; and since I had no other means but loud speaking, the idea of making the learners draw, write, and work at the same time was naturally developed.

The confusion of the repeating crowd led me to feel the need of keeping time, and beating time increased the impression made by the lesson. The utter ignorance of all made me stay long over the beginnings; and this led me to realize the high degree of inner power to be obtained by perfecting the first beginnings, and the result of a feeling of completeness and perfection in the lowest stage. I learned, as never before, the relation of the first steps in every kind of knowledge to its complete outline; and I felt, as never before, the immeasurable gaps that would bear witness in every succeeding stage of knowledge to confusion and want of perfection on these points.

The result of attending to this perfecting of the early stages far outran my expectations. It quickly developed in the children a consciousness of hitherto unknown power, and particularly a general sense of beauty and order. They felt their own power, and the tediousness of the ordinary school-tone vanished like a ghost from my rooms. They wished,—tried,—persevered,—succeeded: and they laughed. Their tone was not that of learners: it was the tone of unknown powers awakened from sleep; of a heart and mind exalted with the feeling of what these powers could and would lead them to do.

Children taught children. They tried to put into practice what I told them to do, and often came themselves on the track of the means of its execution, from many sides. This self-activity, which had developed itself in many ways in the beginning of learning, worked with great force on the birth and growth of the conviction in me, that all true, all educated instruction must be drawn out of the children themselves, and be born within them. To this I was led chiefly by necessity. Since I had no fellow-helpers, I put a capable child between two less capable ones; he embraced them with both arms, he told them what he knew, and they learned to repeat after him what they knew not.[5]

Pestalozzi was requested by a group of supporters of his work, the "Society of the Friends of Education," to prepare for them a basic statement of his method. Although the following selection from "The Method" was not published until after his death, it is useful in providing a formal statement of Pestalozzi's views on teaching method as they had been developed by 1800. Pestalozzi refers to "sense impression of Nature" as "the only true foundation of instruction" and offers eleven "laws" on which teaching practice should be based. When he specifies the use of outcome-shaping stimuli, he appears to conform most closely to the criteria for the Exercise/Imitation Method, although some passages suggest the Discovery/Restructuring Method.

5. Johann Heinrich Pestalozzi, *How Gertrude Teaches Her Children and an Account of the Method,* trans. Lucy E. Holland and Francis C. Turner (Syracuse, N.Y.: C. W. Bardeen, 1898), pp. 39-41, 42-45. All selections from Pestalozzi's *How Gertrude Teaches Her Children* and "The Method" are from this source.

I am trying to psychologize the instruction of mankind; I am trying to bring it into harmony with the nature of my mind, with that of my circumstances and my relations to others. I start from no positive form of teaching, as such, but simply ask myself:—

"What would you do, if you wished to give a single child all the knowledge and practical skill he needs, so that by wise care of his best opportunities he might reach inner content?"

I think to gain this end the human race needs exactly the same thing as the single child.

I think, further, the poor man's child needs a greater refinement in the methods of instruction than the rich man's child.

Nature, indeed, does much for the human race, but we have strayed away from her path. The poor man is thrust away from her bosom, and the rich destroy themselves both by rioting and by lounging on her overflowing breast.

The picture is severe. But ever since I have been able to see I have seen it so; and it is from this view that the impulse arises within me, not merely to plaster over the evils in schools which are enervating the people of Europe, but to cure them at their root.

But this can never be done without subordinating all forms of instruction to those eternal laws by which the human mind is raised from physical impressions on the senses to clear ideas. . . .

Before the child can utter a sound, a many-sided consciousness of all physical truths exists already within him, as a starting-point for the whole round of his experiences. For instance, he feels that the pebble and the tree have different properties; that wood differs from glass. To make this dim consciousness clear, speech is necessary. We must give him names for the various things he knows, as well as for their properties.

So we connect his speech with his knowledge, and extend his knowledge with his speech. This makes the consciousness of impressions which have touched his senses clearer to the child. And the common work of all instruction is to make this consciousness clear.

This may be done in two ways. Either we lead the children through knowledge of names to that of things, or else through knowledge of things to that of names. The second method is mine. I wish always to let sense-impression precede the word, and definite knowledge the judgment. I wish to make words and talk unimportant on the human mind, and to secure that preponderance due to the actual impressions of physical objects . . . that forms such a remarkable protection against mere noise and empty sound. From his very first development I wish to lead my child into the whole circle of Nature surrounding him; I would organize his learning to talk by a collection of natural products; I would teach him early to abstract all physical generalizations from separate physical facts, and teach him to express them in words; and I would everywhere substitute physical generalizations for those metaphysical generalizations with which we begin the instruction of our race. Not till after the foundation of human knowledge (sense-impressions of Nature) has been fairly laid and secure would I begin the dull, abstract work of studying from books. . . .

Words of one or more syllables are placed letter by letter on the board. For instance, take the word Soldatenstand. We first put:—

	S	and	ask,	How	do	you	say	that?	Answer,	S
then	O	"		"		"		now ?	"	SO
"	L	"		"		"		"	"	SOL
"	D	"		"		"		"	"	SOLD
"	A	"		"		"		"	"	SOLDA
"	T	"		"		"		"	"	SOLDAT
"	E	"		"		"		"	"	SOLDATE
"	N	"		"		"		"	"	SOLDATEN
"	ST	"		"		"		"	"	SOLDATENST

and so on.

Frequent repetition of building up the same word is absolutely necessary to make the formation and pronunciation perfectly fluent to the child.

When the children can form and pronounce the word with ease, it should be shown them in syllables, and imitated by them until they feel, themselves, which letters on the board belong to each syllable. I number the syllables, and ask: What is the first, the second, and so on? and out of the order of their sequence—the sixth, the first, the fourth, and so on? Then, for the first time, I let them spell it. Changing the letters of a word to be spelled, taking one or more of

them away, adding others, and dividing it up into false syllables, strengthen the observation of the children, and their
increased power enables them to re-arrange the very hardest
words by themselves.

By this method the formation of words becomes evident to children; their organs of speech are exercised to pronounce the hardest words easily; in a short time they reach
an incredible facility in this business, usually so tiresome;
and from one word often learn a number of independent
words, as in the above example. . . .

In this way, gentlemen, I try to follow in elementary
instruction the mechanical laws by which man rises from
sense-impression to clear ideas.

All Nature is bound to this course of action. She is
bound to rise step by step from the simple beginning.

I follow in her path. If the child knows simple bodies—
air, earth, water, fire,—I show him the effects of these elements on bodies that he knows; and as he learns the properties of several simple bodies, I show him the different effects
obtained by uniting one body to another, and lead him always by the simplest course of sense-impression to the
boundaries of the higher sciences. Everything must be put
into forms that make it possible and easy for any sensible
mother to follow this instruction. But I would also wish that
my children, taught in this way, should not let themselves
be led astray by the presumptuous ignorance of schoolmasters. . . .

But it is time I ended. Gentlemen, this is the first
sketch of my principles and method of instruction, and I
offer it to your free criticism.[6]

PESTALOZZI.

BURGDORF, *June 27th, 1800*

We may infer from the previous selections from Pestalozzi
that his method involved aversive teacher-directed effort producing stimuli. But he wanted the teacher's control to be exercised
with love and understanding for the student. In the first of the
following two selections Pestalozzi indicates that this ideal was not
usually attained in the typical classroom. Where loves is present,

6. Pestalozzi, "The Method," pp. 315-16, 327-28, 331-32, 336.

however, as he affirms in the second selection, "no form of education can fail to succeed."

There are no better teachers than the house, and the father's and mother's love, and the daily labour at home and all the wants and necessities of life. But if the children must needs be sent to school, the schoolmaster should at least be an open-hearted, cheerful, affectionate, and kind man, who would be as a father to the children—a man made on purpose to open children's hearts and their mouths, and to draw forth their understandings as it were from the hindermost corner. In most schools, however, it is just the contrary: the schoolmaster seems as if he was made on purpose to shut up children's mouths and hearts, and to bury their good understandings ever so deep underground. That is the reason why healthy and cheerful children, whose hearts are full of joy and gladness, hardly ever like school. Those that show best at school are the children of whining hypocrites or of conceited parish-officers; stupid dunces, who have no pleasure with other children; these are the bright ornaments of schoolrooms, who hold up their heads among the other children like the wooden king in the ninepins among his eight fellows. But if there is a boy who has too much good sense to keep his eyes for hours together fixed upon a dozen letters which he hates; or a merry girl, who, while the schoolmaster discourses of spiritual life, has all kinds of fun with her hands under the desk, the schoolmaster, in his wisdom, decides that these are the goats who care not for their everlasting salvation.[7]

❊   ❊   ❊   ❊   ❊

The bond of family life is a bond of love. It is the means given by God for awakening the capacity for love in the individual. In its purest form it is the most sublime factor imaginable in the education of our race.

Where love and the capacity for love are present in the domestic circle, one might say beforehand that no form of education can fail to succeed. The child must become good.

7. Johann Heinrich Pestalozzi, "Christopher and Elizabeth," *Pestalozzi's Educational Writings,* ed. J. A. Green (London: Edward Arnold, 1916), pp. 44-45.

One might well-nigh affirm that, whenever a child does not seem to be kind, vigorous, and active, it is because his capacity for love has not found that succour and guidance at home which it should.[8]

We must conclude from our examination of Pestalozzi's views on teaching method that his original contributions to our understanding of instructional method are limited at best. His basic approach was that of the Exercise/Imitation Method. Pestalozzi's emphasis on sense impressions as the primary source of knowledge (which, under the name "object lessons," later came to be identified as the essence of Pestalozzi's method in the United States) is, of course, also found in such earlier writers as Comenius and Rousseau. Our negative conclusion regarding Pestalozzi's role in the development of instructional method should not, however, detract from the significance of his experimental schools, which helped to focus popular attention on the problems and possibilities of making primary schooling available to all children.

Selected Bibliography

COMPAYRÉ, GABRIEL. *Pestalozzi and Elementary Education.* Translated by R. P. Jago. New York: Crowell, 1907.

GUTEK, GERALD L. *Pestalozzi and Education.* New York: Random House, 1968.

MONROE, WILL S. *History of the Pestalozzian Movement in the United States.* Syracuse, N.Y.: C. W. Bardeen, 1907.

PINLOCHE, A. *Pestalozzi, and the Foundations of the Modern Elementary School.* New York: Scribner's, 1901.

SILBER, KATE. *Pestalozzi: The Man and His Work.* London: Routledge and Keegan Paul, 1960.

WALCH, MARY ROMANA. *Pestalozzi and the Pestalozzian Theory of Education: A Critical Study.* Washington: Catholic University Press, 1952.

8. Johann Heinrich Pestalozzi, "Views and Experiences," *Pestalozzi's Educational Writings,* p. 163.

5

Johann Friedrich Herbart

As Comenius is known as the father of modern education, Johann Friedrich Herbart has been called "the father of the modern science of education." The difference between these two designations involves, of course, the term "science": Herbart is credited with being the first to apply the science of psychology to the conduct of education.[1]

Herbart was born in Oldenburg, Germany, on May 4, 1776. In 1802 he took his doctorate at the University of Göttingen, where he remained as a lecturer and later was made a professor. In 1806 he published *The Science of Education*. He moved to the University of Königsberg in 1809 to fill the chair in philosophy previously held by Immanuel Kant; in 1833 he returned to Göttingen. The *Outlines of Educational Doctrine*, which contains Herbart's mature views on education, was published in 1835. Herbart died in Göttingen on August 14, 1841.

Harold Dunkel, a contemporary Herbartian scholar, has questioned whether Herbart's views on teaching are really based on his psychology: "[In Herbart's] pedagogical works the explicit references to psychological theory are much less frequent than those to

---

1. Frederick Eby and Charles F. Arrowood, *The Development of Modern Education* (New York: Prentice-Hall, 1946), pp. 758, 765.

ethical theory. And in both explicit and implicit references, the
pedagogical material was used to illustrate or suggest psychological theory. It was not the other way around; psychology was not
used to predict or explain the pedagogical phenomena. In his
pedagogical works Herbart argued for the most part from the
familiar experience of those who have taught—the distilled wisdom of countless generations of schoolmasters—not from psychological theory."[2]

During his lifetime Herbart's educational views did not attain
much popularity. At the time of his death, as Dunkel points out,
he had "arrived at a set of dead ends. . . . That he should ever become more famous than he was at this point seems scarcely con-
ceivable; but such are the surprises of history."[3]

Herbart acquired his later reputation as an outstanding figure
in the development of instructional method through the popular-
ization of his ideas by his disciples. In the United States the so-
called Herbartian Movement exerted considerable influence on
teacher training and the practice of education during the period
1890-1905. "So far as the mass of American teachers were concerned, it was the Herbartian methodology that was of immediate
interest to teaching. If introduced under proper auspices and at
the right time, the Herbartian methodology of the 'five formal
steps' was a psychologically sound way to structure a lesson plan.
These five formal steps were (1) preparation, (2) presentation,
(3) association, (4) generalization, and (5) application."[4]

What was Herbart's original conception of these steps? Herbart discusses the steps in both *The Science of Education* and *Outlines of Educational Doctrine*. In these sources he identifies only
four steps, which he usually labels (1) clearness, (2) association,
(3) system, and (4) method. The pertinent selection from each of
these works is presented below. The reader should note Herbart's
imprecise use of terms and the generally ambiguous character of
his writing (e.g., in the first selection Herbart uses the term "arrangement" for the term "system," and "course of this order" for

2. Harold B. Dunkel, *Herbart and Education* (New York: Random
House, 1969), p. 98.

3. Harold B. Dunkel, *Herbart and Hebartianism: An Educational
Ghost Story* (Chicago: University of Chicago Press, 1970), p. 207.

4. William M. French, *America's Educational Tradition* (Boston: D.
C. Heath, 1964), p. 132.

"method." In the second selection neither "clearness" nor "method" is adequately explained).

Herbart's views on the use of outcome-shaping stimuli are most fully presented in the second of the following selections. He seems generally to advocate the use of pre-response stimuli. His reference to "systematic presentation" is consonant with the Telling/Showing Method; his statement that pupils should "repeat . . . accurately" suggests the Exercise/Imitation Method; and his recommendation that informal conversation be used "because it gives the pupil an opportunity to test and to change the accidental union of his thoughts, to multiply the links of connection, and to assimilate, after his own fashion, what he has learned" is indicative of the Discovery/Restructuring Method.

> Instruction must follow the rule of giving equal weight in every smallest possible group of its objects to concentration and reflection; that is to say, it must care equally and in regular succession for clearness of every particular, for association of the manifold, for coherent ordering of what is associated, and for a certain practice in progression through this order. Upon this depends the distinctness which must rule in all that is taught. The teacher's greatest difficulty here, perhaps, is to find real particulars—to analyse his own thoughts into their elements. Text books can in this case partly prepare the ground.
>
> If however, instruction handles each little group of objects in this manner, many groups arise in the mind, and each one is grasped by a relative concentration until all are united in a higher reflection. But the union of the groups presupposes the perfect unity of each group. So long, therefore, as it is still possible for the last particular in the content of each group to fall apart from the rest, higher reflection cannot be thought of. But there is above this higher reflection a still higher, and so on indefinitely upwards, to the all-embracing highest, which we seek through the system of systems, but never reach. In earlier years nothing of this can be attempted; youth is always in an intermediate state between concentration and distraction. We must be contented in earlier years with not attempting to give what we call system in the higher sense, but must on the other hand so much the more create clearness in every group; we must

associate the groups the more sedulously and variously, and
be careful that *the approach to the all-embracing reflection
is made equally from all sides.*

Upon this depends the articulation of instruction. The
larger members are composed of smaller, as are the lesser of
the least. In each of the smallest members, four stages of
instruction are to be distinguished; it must provide for Clearness, Association, Arrangement, and the Course of this order.
These grades, which with the smallest members quickly succeed each other, follow one another more slowly, when those
next in comprehensiveness are formed from the smallest
members, and with ever-increasing spaces of time, as higher
steps of reflection have to be climbed.[5]

* * * * *

Some teachers lay great stress on the explication,
step by step, of the smaller and smallest components of the
subject, and insist on a similar reproduction on the part of
the pupils. Others prefer to teach by conversation, and allow
themselves and their pupils great freedom of expression.
Others, again, call especially for the leading thoughts, but
demand that these be given with accuracy and precision,
and in the prescribed order. Others, finally, are not satisfied
until their pupils are self-actively exercising their minds in
systematic thinking.

Various methods of teaching may thus arise; it is not
necessary, however, that one should be habitually employed
to the exclusion of the rest. We may ask rather whether each
does not contribute its share to a many-sided culture. In
order that a multitude of facts may be apprehended, expli-
cations or analyses are needed to prevent confusion; but
since a synthesis is equally essential, the latter process may
be started by conversation, continued by lifting into promi-
nence the cardinal thoughts, and completed by the methodical independent thinking of the pupil: *clearness, association,
system, method.*

On closer inspection we find that instead of being mutually exclusive, these various modes of instruction are

5. Johann Friedrich Herbart, *The Science of Education,* trans. Henry
M. and Emmie Felkin (Boston: D. C. Heath, 1908), pp. 144-145. Emphasis in the
original.

requisite, one by one, in the order given above, for every group, small or large, of subjects to be taught.

For, first, the beginner is able to advance but slowly. For him the shortest steps are the safest steps. He must stop at each point as long as is necessary to make him apprehend distinctly each individual fact. To this he must give his whole thought. During the initial stage, the teacher's art consists, therefore, preeminently in knowing how to resolve his subject into very small parts. In this way he will avoid taking sudden leaps without being aware that he is doing so.

Secondly, association cannot be effected solely by a systematic mode of treatment, least of all at first. In the system each part has its own fixed place. At this place it is connected directly with the nearest other parts, but also separated from other more remote parts by a definite distance, and connected with these only by way of determinate intervening members, or links. Besides, the nature of this connection is not the same everywhere. Furthermore, a system is not to be learned merely. It is to be used, applied, and often needs to be supplemented by additions inserted in appropriate places. To be able to do this requires skill in diverting one's thoughts from any given starting-point to every other point, forward, backward, sideways. Hence two things are requisite; preparation for the system, and application of the system. Preparation is involved in association; exercise in systematic thinking must follow.

During the first stage, when the clear apprehension of the individual object or fact is the main thing, the shortest and most familiar words and sentences are the most appropriate. The teacher will often find it advisable also to have some, if not all, of the pupils repeat them accurately after him. As is well known, even speaking in concert has been tried in many schools not entirely without success, and for young beginners this method may indeed at times answer very well.

For association, the best mode of procedure is informal conversation, because it gives the pupil an opportunity to test and to change the accidental union of his thoughts, to multiply the links of connection, and to assimilate, after his own fashion, what he has learned. It enables him, besides, to do at least a part of all this in any way that happens to be the easiest and most convenient. He will thus escape the inflexibility of thought that results from a purely systematic learning.

System, on the other hand, calls for a more connected discourse, and the period of presentation must be separated more sharply from the period of repetition. By exhibiting and emphasizing the leading principles, system impresses upon the minds of pupils the value of organized knowledge; through its greater completeness it enriches their store of information. But pupils are incapable of appreciating either advantage when the systematic presentation is introduced too early.

Skill in systematic thinking the pupil will obtain through the solution of assigned tasks, his own independent attempts, and their correction. For such work will show whether he has fully grasped the general principles, and whether he is able to recognize them in and apply them to particulars.

These remarks on the initial analysis and the subsequent gradual uniting of the matter taught, hold true, in general and in detail, of the most diverse objects and branches of instruction. Much remains to be added, however, to define with precision the application of these principles to a given subject and to the age of the pupil.[6]

Herbart believed that overtly provided, aversive effort-producing stimuli were an essential element in the teaching process. This view is expressed in the following two selections.

Education proper is cognisant, like government, of something which may be called compulsion; it is indeed never harsh, but often very strict. . . .

Education makes itself quite as oppressive, though less abruptly so, by constantly exacting that which is unwillingly done, and by obstinately ignoring the wishes of the pupil. In this, as in the former case, the teacher reminds the pupil in silence, or, if necessary, aloud, of the pre-existing contract: "Our relationship exists and endures only on such and such conditions." This, it must be admitted, has no meaning if the teacher does not know how to secure for himself a cer-

6. Johann Friedrich Herbart, *Outlines of Educational Doctrine*, trans. Alexis F. Lange (New York: Macmillan, 1901), pp. 52-57. Emphasis in the original.

tain free position. This is soon followed by the withdrawal of the customary signs of courtesy and approbation. Such customary signs presuppose that as a rule the pupil will be treated as a human being, with ordinary kindness, and perhaps, as a lovable boy, with all the affectionate sympathy he deserves. This includes the yet wider presumption that the teacher has taste and a feeling for all the beauty and attractiveness that humanity and youth may possess. The sour-tempered person who is insensible to this feeling would do better to avoid the young—he does not so much as understand how to look at them with proper consideration. Only he who receives much, and is therefore able to give much, can also deprive of much, and by such pressure mould the disposition and direct the attention of the youthful mind according to his own judgment.[7]

❀   ❀   ❀   ❀   ❀

Child government, to be effective, requires both gentle and severe measures. In general, this effectiveness results from the natural superiority of the adult, a fact of which teachers sometimes need to be reminded. Whatever the plan of supervision, there must be coupled with it an adequate mode of disciplinary procedure. A record should be kept in schools, not for the law-abiding pupils, but for those guilty of repeated acts of disobedience. These remarks do not thus far include any reference to marks and records pertaining to education proper; they are confined to what is popularly, but loosely, called discipline, that is, the training of pupils to conform to the system of order that obtains in the school.

It would be in vain to attempt to banish entirely the corporal punishments usually administered after fruitless reprimands; but use should be made of them so sparingly that they be feared rather than actually inflicted.

Recollection of the rod does not hurt a boy. Nor is there any harm in his present conviction that a flogging is henceforth as much beyond the range of possibility as his meriting such treatment. But it would, no doubt, be injurious to actually violate his self-respect by a blow, however little he might mind the physical pain. And pernicious in the

7. Herbart, *The Science of Education*, pp. 103, 103-104.

highest degree, although, nevertheless, not quite obsolete yet, is the practice of continuing to beat children already hardened to blows. Brutish insensibility is the consequence, and the hope is almost vain that even a long period of now unavoidable indulgence will restore a normal state of feeling.

There is less objection to making use, for a few hours, of hunger as a corrective. Here only an act of deprivation takes place, not one involving a direct insult.

Curtailment of freedom is the most commonly employed form of punishment; justly so, provided it be properly adjusted to the offence. Moreover, it admits of the most varied gradations from standing in a corner to confinement in a dark room, perhaps even with hands tied together behind the back. Only, for several serious reasons, this punishment must not be of long duration. A whole hour is more than enough unless there is careful supervision. Besides, the place must be chosen judiciously.

Corrections of such severity, as removal from home or expulsion from an institution, are to be administered only in extreme cases; for what is to become of the expelled pupil? A burden to another school? And in case the transfer implies the same freedom, the old disorderly conduct will usually be resumed. Such pupils must, therefore, be placed under very strict supervision and given new occupations. We must trust to the new environment to obliterate gradually the old vitiated circle of thought.

It is a well-known fact that authority and love are surer means of securing order than harsh measures are. But authority cannot be created by every one at will. It implies obvious superiority in mind, in knowledge, in physique, in external circumstances. Love can, indeed, be gained in the course of time by a complaisant manner—the love of well-disposed pupils; but just where government becomes most necessary, complaisance has to cease. Love must not be purchased at the expense of weak indulgence; it is of value only when united with the necessary severity.[8]

Based on the preceding selections, we would have to classify Herbart's views as representing one or more of the traditional conceptions of teaching method. Therefore, we must assess his con-

8. Herbart, *Outlines of Educational Doctrine*, pp. 33-35.

tribution to instructional method to be relatively unoriginal and essentially an elaboration of a traditional view.

Herbart's steps do not represent his only statements on teaching method, however. His works also contain numerous practical suggestions for teachers, as illustrated by the excerpt given below (in this case the method described is another traditional one—the Exercise/Imitation Method). How are these other ideas to be assessed? As Dunkel says, they are "largely the prescription of the personal preferences of the educator in question—granted that like all such prescriptions past and present they may rest on experience which the educator has sought to examine. They are, to be sure, better organized and set forth in greater detail than the observations of most of his predecessors. But if this is all that Herbart has to offer as the 'father of scientific education'; then he was not even a ghost, but rather the figment of various imaginations, of which his own was the first."[9]

> Many pupils have to be shown how to memorize. Left to themselves they will begin over and over again, then halt, and try in vain to go on. A fundamental rule is that the starting-point be shifted. If, for example, the name Methuselah is to be learned, the teacher would, perhaps, say successively: lah,—selah,—thuselah,—Methuselah.
>
> Some have to be warned against trying to get through quickly. We have to do here with a physical mechanism which requires time and whose operation the pupil himself as little as the teacher should endeavor to over-accelerate. Slow at first, then faster.
>
> It is not always advisable to put a stop to all bodily movements. Many memorize by way of speaking aloud, others through copying, some through drawing. Reciting in concert also may prove feasible at times.
>
> Incorrect associations are very much to be feared; they are tenacious. A great deal, to be sure, may be accomplished through severity; but when interest in the subject-matter is wholly lacking, the pupil begins by memorizing incorrectly, then ceases to memorize at all, and simply wastes time.
>
> The absolute failure of some pupils in memory work may perhaps be partly owing to unknown physical peculiari-

9. Dunkel, *Herbart and Herbartianism*, pp. 206-207.

ties. Very often, however, the cause of the evil lies in the state of false tension into which such pupils put themselves while attempting with reluctance what they regard as an almost impossible task. A teacher's injudicious attitude during the first period, his remarks, for instance, about learning by heart as a thing of toil and trouble, may lead to this state of mind, for which perhaps awkward first steps in learning to read have prepared the way. It is foolish to look for means of lightening still more the exercises of children that retain and recite with facility; but, on the other hand, great caution is necessary because there are also others who may be rendered unfit for memorizing by the first attempt of the teacher to make them recite, or even only to repeat after him, a certain series of words. In attempting, by such early tests, to find out whether children retain and reproduce easily, it is essential that the teacher put them in good humor, that he select his matter with this end in view, and that he go on only so long as they feel they can do what is asked of them. The results of his observations must determine the further mode of procedure.

However carefully the process of memorizing may have been performed, the question remains: How long will the memorized matter be retained? On this point teachers deceive themselves time and again, in spite of universally common experiences.

Now, in the first place, not everything that is learned by heart needs to be retained. Many an exercise serves its purpose when it prepares the way for the next, and renders further development possible. In this way a short poem is sometimes learned as a temporary means for an exercise in declamation; or chapters from Latin authors are committed to memory in order to speed the writing and speaking of Latin. In many cases it is sufficient for later years if the pupil knows how to look for literary helps, and how to make use of them.

But if, secondly, that which has been memorized is to remain impressed on the memory for a long time, forever if possible, it is only a questionable expedient to reassign the same thing as often as it is forgotten. The feeling of weary disgust may more than offset the possible gain. There is only one efficient method—practice.[10]

[10]Herbart, *Outlines of Educational Doctrine*, pp. 72-75.

Selected Bibliography

COMPAYRÉ, G. *Herbart and Education by Instruction.* New York: Crowell, 1907.

DeGARMO, CHARLES. *Herbart and the Herbartians.* New York: Scribner's, 1895.

DUNKEL, HAROLD B. *Herbart and Herbartianism: An Educational Ghost Story.* Chicago: University of Chicago Press, 1970.

DUNKEL, HAROLD B. *Herbart and Education.* New York: Random House, 1969.

FELKIN, F. M. and FELKIN, E. *An Introduction to Herbart's Science and Practice of Education.* Boston: D. C. Heath, 1895.

6

Friedrich Froebel

It is generally held that the three most outstanding figures in the development of teaching method during the nineteenth century were Pestalozzi, Herbart, and Friedrich Froebel. Froebel is famous as the developer of the kindergarten and for the use of special instructional materials (which he called "gifts").

Froebel was born on April 21, 1782, in Oberweissbach, Germany; he died on June 21, 1852, in Marienthal. In 1799 he went to the University of Jena, but he did not complete his studies. In 1805 Froebel began a career in teaching, which was to occupy the rest of his life. His first important work on education, *The Education of Man*, was published in 1826. In 1837 Froebel opened the first kindergarten in Blankenburg. He spent his remaining years furthering the kindergarten concept. The major statement of his ideas on the kindergarten is contained in a series of essays written between 1837 and 1840, which were collected and published posthumously in 1861 as the *Pedagogics of the Kindergarten*.

Froebel's views on the use of outcome-shaping stimuli encompass the three traditional conceptions of instructional method. It is difficult, however, to isolate his specific ideas owing to a writing style that is effusive and imprecise. The following selection from *The Education of Man* illustrates both his manner of presentation and his eclectic approach to teaching.

The aim and object of the parental care of the child, in the domestic and family circle, then, is to awaken and develop, to quicken all the powers and natural gifts of the child, to enable all the members and organs of man to fulfill the requirements of the child's powers and gifts.

The natural mother does all this instinctively, without instruction and direction; but this is not enough: it is needful that she should do it consciously, as a conscious being acting upon another being which is growing into consciousness . . . and consciously tending toward the continuous development of the human being, in a certain inner living connection.

By sketching her work, therefore, I hope to show it to her in its nature, significance, and connection. It is true, the plainest thoughtful mother could do this more fully, more perfectly, and more deeply; but through imperfection man rises to perfection. I trust, therefore, that this sketch may awaken faithful and calm, thoughtful and rational parental love, and show us the course of development in childhood in unbroken succession.

"Give me your arm." "Where is your hand?" In such words the mother strives to teach the child to feel the complexity of his body and the difference between his limbs.

"Bite your finger." This is an especially well-conceived action, which a deep natural feeling has suggested to the thoughtful mother playing with her child. It induces reflection in its earliest phases, by tending to bring to the child's knowledge an object which, although it has an individuality of its own, is yet united with the child.

Not less important is the mother's pleasantly playful manner of leading the child to a knowledge of the members which he can not *see*, the nose, the ears, the tongue, and teeth. The mother gently pulls the nose or ear, as if she meant to separate them from head or face, and, showing to the child the half-concealed end of her finger or thumb, says, "Here I have the ear, the nose," and the child quickly puts his hand to his ear or nose, and smiles with intense joy to find them in their right places. In this action the mother first arouses and directs in the child a desire to know even what he can not see externally.

All this tends to lead the child to self-consciousness, to reflection about himself in the approaching period of boyhood. Thus, a boy ten years old, similarly guided by instinct, believing himself unobserved, soliloquized: "I am not my arm, nor my ear; all my limbs and organs I can separate from myself, and I still remain myself; I wonder what I am; who and what this is which I call myself?"

In the same spirit, maternal love continues with the child, in order to lead him to use these things. "Show me your tongue." "Show me your tooth." "Bite it with your tooth." "Slip the foot into the stocking—into the shoe." "There is the foot in the stocking—in the shoe."

Thus maternal instinct and love gradually introduce the child to his little outside world, proceeding from the whole to the part, from the near to the remote. . . .

Behold here the little child of the gardener. He is weeding; the child wishes to help, and he teaches the little fellow to distinguish hemlock from parsley, to observe the differences in the brilliancy and odor of the leaves.

There the forester's son accompanies his father to the clearing that, at some previous time, they together had sown. Everything looks green. The child sees only young pine-plants; but the father teaches him to recognize the cypress-spurge and to distinguish it from the pine-plant by its different properties.

Again, the father takes aim and fires; he hits the mark, and teaches the attentive child that three points that lie in the same direction always lie in one and the same straight line; that in order to direct a line—the barrel of the rifle—toward a certain point, three points must be laid in this direction, and that, when this has been done, all other points of the gun-barrel lie in the same line and direction.

In another place the child sees his father striking the hot iron, and is taught by the father that the heat makes the iron softer; and, again, as the father tries in vain to push the heated iron rod through an opening through which before it passed so easily, that heat expands the iron.

The child—your child, ye fathers—feels this so intensely, so vividly, that he follows you wherever you are, wherever you go, in whatever you do. Do not harshly repel him; show no impatience about his ever-recurring questions. Every harshly repelling word crushes a bud or shoot of his tree of life. Do not, however, tell him in words much more than he could find himself without your words. For it is, of course, easier to hear the answer from another, perhaps to only half hear and understand it, than it is to seek and discover it himself. To have found one fourth of the answer by his own effort is of more value and importance to the child than it is to half hear and half understand it in the words of another; for this causes mental indolence. Do not, therefore, always answer your children's questions at once and directly; but, *as soon as they have gathered sufficient strength and experience,* furnish them with the means to find the answers in the sphere of their own knowledge.

Let parents—more particularly fathers (for to their special care and guidance the child ripening into boyhood is confided)—let fathers contemplate what the fulfillment of their paternal duties in child-guidance yields to them; let them feel the joys it brings. It is not possible to gain from anything higher joy, higher enjoyment, than we do from the guidance of our children, from living with and for our children. It is inconceivable how we can seek and expect to find anywhere higher joy, higher enjoyment, fuller gratification of our best desires than we can find in intercourse with our children; more recreation than we can find in the family circle, where we can create joy for ourselves in so many respects.

We should be deeply impressed with the truth of these statements could we but see in his plain home-surroundings, in his happy, joyous family, the father who, from his own resources, has created what here has been but partially described. In a few words he sums up his rule of conduct: "To lead children early to think, this I consider the first and foremost object of child-training."

To give them early habits of work and industry seemed to him so natural and obvious a course as to need no statement in words. Besides, the child that has been led to think will thereby, at the same time, be led to industry, dilligence —to all domestic and civic virtues.[1]

Froebel's views on the source of effort-producing stimuli are quite clear, however. The excerpt below presents his general conception of the need for aversive teacher control.

1. Friedrich Froebel, *The Education of Man,* trans. W. N. Hailmann (New York: Appleton, 1887), pp. 64-66, 85-87. Emphasis in the original.

Real discipline . . . is the very centre of education in boyhood. . . . Discipline implies that the boy in all his actions respects his own human nature because he realizes its dignity and worth. The more clearly he recognizes the requirements of his true humanity, the more definitely and firmly should the educator insist on the fulfilment of those requirements. He should not even shrink from severity and infliction of punishment if the good of the pupil demand it; for boyhood is the time for discipline.[2]

Central to Froebel's conception of teaching is the use of geometric objects. Such objects, which he calls "gifts," are presented to the child; and it is through manipulation of the gift and playing with it that he acquires the desired learning outcomes. In the following selection from *Pedagogics of the Kindergarten* Froebel describes the use of the first gift, the ball. Because of the use of such terms as "new perception," this excerpt would seem to exemplify the use of the Discovery/Restructuring Method.

As soon as the child is sufficiently developed to perceive the ball as a thing separate from himself, it will be easy for you, dear mother, and you, dear nurse, having previously fastened a string to the ball which you give into the child's little hand, to draw the ball gently by the string as if you wished to lift it out of the child's little hand. The child will hold the ball fast, the arm will rise as you lift the ball, and as you loosen the string the hand and arm will sink back from their own weight and through holding the ball fast; the feeling of the utterance of force, as well as the alternation of the movement, will soon delight the child; and the use of the arm in this activity gives dexterity to the arm and strengthens the arm and hand.

Now, dear mother, here is the beginning of your play and playing with your dear child through the mediation of the ball. From this, however, soon springs a quite new play, and thus also something new to the child, when, through a suitable drawing and lifting by the string, the ball escapes from the child's hand, and then quietly moves freely before him as an individual object. Through this play is developed

2. S. S. F. Fletcher and J. Welton, *Froebel's Chief Writings on Education* (New York: Longmans, Green, 1912), pp. 95, 95.

in the child the new feeling, the new perception of the object as a something now clasped, grasped, and handled, and now a freely active, opposite something.

One may say with deep conviction that even this simple activity is inexpressively important for the child, for which reason it is to be repeated as a play with the child as often as possible. What the little one has up to this time directly felt so often by the touch of the mother's breast—union and separation—it now perceives outwardly in an object which can be grasped and clasped, and which has actually been grasped and clasped. Thus the repetition of this play confirms, strengthens, and clears up in the mind of the child a feeling and perception deeply grounded in and important to the whole life of man—the feeling and perception of oneness and individuality, and of disjunction and separateness; also of present and past possession.

It is exceedingly important for the child which is to be developed, as well as for the adults who are to develop him (therefore, first of all, for the father and mother), that they (the adults) should not only perceive but should also suitably foster the awakening individual power and individual activity, and the awakening spirit of their child in the traces and slightest expressions found in the almost imperceptible beginning, so that the development of these qualities and this spirit may not be carried on by accidental, arbitrary, and disconnected exercises. It is also important to observe the progressive development of the strength as well as of the activity by means of a measuring object, for which also the play with the ball is in manifold ways the most suitable means for parents and child.

The idea of return or recurrence soon develops to the child's perception from the presence and absence; that of reunion, from the singleness and separateness; that of future repossession, from present and past possession; and so the ideas of being, having, and becoming are most important to the whole life of man in their results, and are therefore the dim perceptions which first dawn on the child.

From these perceptions there at once develop in the child's mind the three great perceptions of object, space, and time, which were at first one collective perception. From the perceptions of being, having, and becoming in respect to space and object, and in connection with them, there soon

develop also the new perceptions of present, past, and future
in respect to time. Indeed, these ninefold perceptions which
open to the child the portals of a new objective life, unfold
themselves most clearly to the child by means of his constant
play with the one single ball.[3]

Another important element in Froebel's conception of teaching method is the use of play. The following selection from *Pedagogics of the Kindergarten* illustrates the use of this technique. In
this selection the teaching method portrayed would appear to be
Exercise/Imitation.

That not only the strength called into activity
leads to the constant development of the whole life, but that
the strength adjusted in every direction to the requirements
of life, so as to produce a harmony, has the same result, can
be taught to the child by the simple play in which the ball
is thrown down to a level plane surface, and bounding from
this perpendicularly into the air, is driven back again and
again by the flat hand to the plane surface. This play can be
accompanied by the words sung or spoken by the child, or
by the attentive teacher:

Spring! spring! spring!
You are a brave thing;
On the ground you will not lie,
Always up from it you fly.
Your own force,
Does, of course,
Take you up so high.

The child not only finds outside of himself in play, indeed by his play, and indeed by his plaything the ball (although it be a so-called lifeless body), that use of the
strength increases the strength, and that orderly employment
of the strength prolongs its use; but he perceives this fact of
his own accord, and as a fact of his own nature, and not
merely as an external fact limited in its application to his
play or to his plaything. Therefore the child now likes to

3. Friedrich Froebel, *Pedagogics of the Kindergarten*, trans. Josephine
Jarvis (New York: Appleton, 1900), pp. 36-39.

sing at each suitable opportunity to its ball, playing with it at the same time:

How much my ball I prize !
My strength I exercise—
All my strength on thee.
Joy thou bringest me.

To catch thee I must try
Quickly to spring, and high.
If I can succeed,
I am glad, indeed.

When to catch I'm ready,
Must my eye be steady,
And, in glad play, see
No other aim than thee.

My hollowed hands I learn
Always to thee to turn ;
If thou dost in them fall,
How glad I am, my ball !

How much my ball I prize !
My strength I exercise—
All my strength on thee.
Dear ball, stay with me!

Hence the meaning of the play is to apply a similar procedure to a solution of the highest problem of life, and *to hold fast the one high purpose amid all the vicissitudes of time and place.*[4]

Selected Bibliography

KILPATRICK, WILLIAM H. *Froebel's Kindergarten Principles Critically Examined.* New York: Macmillan, 1916.

LILLEY, IRENE M. *Friedrich Froebel: A Selection from His Writings.* Cambridge: Cambridge University Press, 1967.

WEBER, EVELYN. *The Kindergarten: Its Encounter with Educational Thought in America.* New York: Teachers College Press, 1969.

4. *Ibid.*, pp. 158-159. Emphasis in the original.

7

John Dewey

John Dewey was one of the dominant figures in twenttieth century education. Through the influence of his writings and the work of his disciples, his name has become associated with much of what is claimed to be good or bad in American education today.

Dewey was born in Burlington, Vermont, on October 20, 1859, and died in New York on June 1, 1952. Dewey graduated from the University of Vermont in 1879. After an additional year of study at the university and a brief interval as a school teacher, he entered Johns Hopkins University. He earned his Ph.D. degree in 1884 and accepted a position as instructor in philosophy at the University of Michigan in the same year. Ten years later he went to the University of Chicago, where he helped to develop its "Laboratory School." From 1904 until his retirement in 1930 he was a professor of philosophy at Columbia University. Dewey published numerous works in philosophy throughout his lifetime. Among his major writings on education are *The School and Society* (1899), *The Child and the Curriculum* (1902), *Democracy and Education* (1916), and *Experience and Education* (1938).

Dewey's basic view of the teaching process is that the student must be an active learner. As far as outcome-shaping stimuli are concerned, his position is compatible with either the Exercise/

86

Imitation Method or the Discovery/Restructuring Method. In the
following two selections (the first from *School and Society* and
the second from *Democracy and Education*), the terms "exercise"
and "discovery" are both used.

The statement so frequently made that education
means "drawing out" is excellent, if we mean simply to con-
trast it with the process of pouring in. But, after all, it is difficult to connect the idea of drawing out with the ordinary
doings of the child of three, four, seven, or eight years of
age. He is already running over, spilling over, with activities
of all kinds. He is not a purely latent being whom the adult
has to approach with great caution and skill in order gradually to draw out some hidden germ of activity. The child
is already intensely active, and the question of education is
the question of taking hold of his activities, of giving them
direction. Through direction, through organized use, they
tend toward valuable results, instead of scattering or being
left to merely impulsive expression.

If we keep this before us, the difficulty I find upper-
most in the minds of many people regarding what is termed
the new education is not so much solved as dissolved; it dis-
appears. A question often asked is: if you begin with the
child's ideas, impulses and interests, all so crude, so random
and scattering, so little refined or spiritualized, how is he
going to get the necessary discipline, culture and information? If there were no way open to us except to excite and
indulge these impulses of the child, the question might well
be asked. We should either have to ignore and repress the
activities, or else to humor them. But if we have organization
of equipment and of materials, there is another path open to
us. We can direct the child's activities, giving them exercise
along certain lines, and can thus lead up to the goal which
logically stands at the end of the paths followed.[1]

❄   ❄   ❄   ❄   ❄

Speaking generally, the fundamental fallacy in
methods of instruction lies in supposing that experience on
the part of pupils may be assumed. What is here insisted

1. John Dewey, *The School and Society* (Chicago: University of Chicago Press, 1899), pp. 53-54.

upon is the necessity of an actual empirical situation as the initiating phase of thought. Experience is here taken as previously defined: trying to do something and having the thing perceptibly do something to one in return. The fallacy consists in supposing that we can begin with ready-made subject matter of arithmetic, or geography, or whatever, irrespective of some direct personal experience of a situation. Even the kindergarten and Montessori techniques are so anxious to get at intellectual distinctions, without "waste of time," that they tend to ignore—or reduce—the immediate crude handling of the familiar material of experience, and to introduce pupils at once to material which expresses the intellectual distinctions which adults have made. But the first stage of contact with any new material, at whatever age of maturity, must inevitably be of the trial and error sort. An individual must actually try, in play or work, to do something with material in carrying out his own impulsive activity, and then note the interaction of his energy and that of the material employed. This is what happens when a child at first begins to build with blocks, and it is equally what happens when a scientific man in his laboratory begins to experiment with unfamiliar objects.

Hence the first approach to any subject in school, if thought is to be aroused and not words acquired, should be as unscholastic as possible. To realize what an experience, or empirical situation, means, we have to call to mind the sort of situation that presents itself outside of school; the sort of occupations that interest and engage activity in ordinary life. And careful inspection of methods which are permanently successful in formal education, whether in arithmetic or learning to read, or studying geography, or learning physics or a foreign language, will reveal that they depend for their efficiency upon the fact that they go back to the type of the situation which causes reflection out of school in ordinary life. They give the pupils something to do, not something to learn; and the doing is of such a nature as to demand thinking, or the intentional noting of connections; learning naturally results.

That the situation should be of such a nature as to arouse thinking means of course that it should suggest something to do which is not either routine or capricious—something, in other words, presenting what is new (and hence uncertain or problematic) and yet sufficiently connected with existing habits to call out an effective response. An effective response means one which accomplishes a perceptible result, in distinction from a purely haphazard activity, where the consequences cannot be mentally connected with what is done. The most significant question which can be asked, accordingly, about any situation or experience proposed to induce learning is what quality of problem it involves. . . .

The perplexing situation must be sufficiently like situations which have already been dealt with so that pupils will have some control of the means of handling it. A large part of the art of instruction lies in making the difficulty of new problems large enough to challenge thought, and small enough so that, in addition to the confusion naturally attending the novel elements, there shall be luminous familiar spots from which helpful suggestions may spring. . . .

The child of three who discovers what can be done with blocks, or of six who finds out what he can make by putting five cents and five cents together, is really a discoverer, even though everybody else in the world knows it. There is a genuine increment of experience; not another item mechanically added on, but enrichment by a new quality. The charm which the spontaneity of little children has for sympathetic observers is due to perception of this intellectual originality. The joy which children themselves experience is the joy of intellectual constructiveness—of creativeness, if the word may be used without misundertanding.

The educational moral I am chiefly concerned to draw is not, however, that teachers would find their own work less of a grind and strain if school conditions favored learning in the sense of discovery and not in that of storing away what others pour into them; nor that it would be possible to give even children and youth the delights of personal intellectual productiveness—true and important as are these things. It is that no thought, no idea, can possibly be conveyed as an idea from one person to another. When it is told, it is, to the one to whom it is told, another given fact, not an idea. The communication may stimulate the other person to realize the question for himself and to think out a like idea, or it may smother his intellectual interest and suppress his dawning effort at thought. But what he *directly* gets cannot be an

idea. Only by wrestling with the conditions of the problem
at first hand, seeking and finding his own way out, does he
think. When the parent or teacher has provided the conditions which stimulate thinking and has taken a sympathetic
attitude toward the activities of the learner by entering into
a common or conjoint experience, all has been done which a
second party can do to instigate learning. The rest lies with
the one directly concerned. If he cannot devise his own solution (not of course in isolation, but in correspondence with
the teacher and other pupils) and find his own way out he
will not learn, not even if he can recite some correct answer
with one hundred per cent accuracy. We can and do supply
ready-made "ideas" by the thousand; we do not usually take
much pains to see that the one learning engages in significant situations where his own activities generate, support,
and clinch ideas—that is, perceived meanings or connections.
This does not mean that the teacher is to stand off and look
on; the alternative to furnishing ready-made subject matter
and listening to the accuracy with which it is reproduced is
not quiescence, but participation, sharing, in an activity.[2]

Dewey's conception of teaching method gives considerable
attention to the question of how to secure student involvement in
the instructional process. The first excerpt below (from *The Child
and the Curriculum*) expresses Dewey's idea that the student
should have a genuine interest in what he is to learn, and that this
interest will be present if "the subject-matter of the lessons be such
as to have an appropriate place within the expanding consciousness of the child, if it grows out of his own past doings, thinkings,
and sufferings, and grows into application in further achievements
and receptivities." Dewey is critical in this selection of three other
techniques of motivating students (the first two of these make use
of overtly provided, aversive effort-producing stimuli; the third
technique depends upon student-originated effort-producing stimuli, but Dewey considers it to be a "trick of method" because the
material to be learned has been "sugar-coated" rather than "psychologized"—that is, developed "within the range and scope of the
child's life.") In the second selection (from *Experience and Educa-*

2. John Dewey, *Democracy and Education* (New York: Macmillan,
1916), pp. 180-82, 184, 187-88. Emphasis in the original.

tion) Dewey expresses his later views on the same topic. He seems to favor some kind of overt (aversive) teacher direction for the student, yet he also seems to want the student to decide what and when he should learn. Moreover, Dewey appears to take for granted the fact that the child will be in the classroom; hence he presumably favors compulsory schooling. We believe, therefore, that his later conception of teaching method more closely resembles the traditional methods than it does the Student Interest Method originated by Rousseau, whereas in his earlier view he he apparently rejected most forms of aversive control.

Somehow and somewhere motive must be appealed to, connection must be established between the mind and its material. There is no question of getting along without this bond of connection; the only question is whether it be such as grows out of the material itself in relation to the mind, or be imported and hitched on from some outside source. If the subject-matter of the lessons be such as to have an appropriate place within the expanding consciousness of the child, if it grows out of his own past doings, thinkings, and sufferings, and grows into application in further achievements and receptivities, then no device or trick of method has to be resorted to in order to enlist "interest." The psychologized *is* of interest—that is, it is placed in the whole of conscious life so that it shares the worth of that life. But the externally presented material, that, conceived and generated in standpoints and attitudes remote from the child, and developed in motives alien to him, has no such place of its own. Hence the recourse to adventitious leverage to push it in, to factitious drill to drive it in, to artificial bribe to lure it in.

Three aspects of this recourse to outside ways for giving the subject-matter some psychological meaning may be worth mentioning. Familiarity breeds contempt, but it also breeds something like affection. We get used to the chains we wear, and we miss them when removed. 'Tis an old story that through custom we finally embrace what at first wore a hideous mien. Unpleasant, because meaningless, activities may get agreeable if long enough persisted in. *It is possible for the mind to develop interest in a routine or mechanical procedure, if conditions are continually supplied which de-*

mand that mode of operation and preclude any other sort.
I frequently hear dulling devices and empty exercises de-
fended and extolled because "the children take such an
'interest' in them." Yes, that is the worst of it; the mind, shut
out from worthy employ and missing the taste of adequate
performance, comes down to the level of that which is left
to it to know and do, and perforce takes an interest in a
cabined and cramped experience. To find satisfaction in its
own exercise is the normal law of mind, and if large and
meaningful business for the mind be denied, it tries to content itself with the formal movements that remain to it—and
too often succeeds, save in those cases of more intense activity which cannot accommodate themselves, and that make
up the unruly and *declassé* of our school product. An interest
in the formal apprehension of symbols and in their memorized reproduction becomes in many pupils a substitute for
the original and vital interest in reality and all because, the
subject-matter of the course of study being out of relation
to the concrete mind of the individual, some substitute bond
to hold it in some kind of working relation to the mind must
be discovered and elaborated.

The second substitute for living motivation in the subject-matter is that of contrast-effects; the material of the
lesson is rendered interesting, if not in itself, at least in con-
trast with some alternative experience. To learn the lesson
is more interesting than to take a scolding, be held up to
general ridicule, stay after school, receive degradingly low
marks, or fail to be promoted. And very much of what goes
by the name of "discipline," and prides itself upon opposing
the doctrines of a soft pedagogy and upon upholding the
banner of effort and duty, is nothing more or less than just
this appeal to "interest" in its obverse aspect—to fear, to dislike of various kinds of physical, social, and personal pain.
The subject-matter does not appeal; it cannot appeal; it lacks
origin and bearing in a growing experience. So the appeal
is to the thousand and one outside and irrelevent agencies
which may serve to throw, by sheer rebuff and rebound,
the mind back upon the material from which it is constantly
wandering.

Human nature being what it is, however, it tends to
seek its motivation in the agreeable rather than in the disagreeable, in direct pleasure rather than in alternative pain.

And so has come up the modern theory and practice of the "interesting," in the false sense of that term. The material is still left; so far as its own characteristics are concerned, just material externally selected and formulated. It is still just so much geography and arithmetic and grammar study; not so much potentiality of child-experience with regard to language, earth, and numbered and measured reality. Hence the difficulty of bringing the mind to bear upon it; hence its repulsiveness; the tendency for attention to wander; for other acts and images to crowd in and expel the lesson. The legitimate way out is to transform the material; to psychologize it—that is . . . to take it and to develop it within the range and scope of the child's life. But it is easier and simpler to leave it as it is, and then by trick of method to *arouse* interest, to *make* it *interesting*; to cover it with sugar-coating; to conceal its barrenness by intermediate and unrelated material; and finally, as it were, to get the child to swallow and digest the unpalatable morsel while he is enjoying tasting something quite different. But alas for the analogy! Mental assimilation is a matter of consciousness; and if the attention has not been playing upon the actual material, that has not been apprehended, nor worked into faculty. . . .

[It is fallacious to assume] that we have no choice save either to leave the child to his own unguided spontaneity or to inspire direction upon him from without. Action is response; it is adaptation, adjustment. There is no such thing as sheer self-activity possible—because all activity takes place in a medium, in a situation, and with reference to its conditions. But, again, no such thing as imposition of truth from without, as insertion of truth from without, is possible. All depends upon the activity which the mind itself undergoes in responding to what is presented from without.[3]

❊   ❊   ❊   ❊   ❊

Traditional education tended to ignore the importance of personal impulse and desire as moving springs. But this is no reason why progressive education should identify impulse and desire with purpose and thereby pass lightly over the need for careful observation, for wide range of

3. John Dewey, *The Child and the Curriculum* (Chicago: University of Chicago Press, 1902), pp. 34-38, 39. Emphasis in the original.

information, and for judgment if students are to share in the formation of the purposes which activate them. In an *educational* scheme, the occurrence of a desire and impulse is not the final end. It is an occasion and a demand for the formation of a plan and method of activity. Such a plan, to repeat, can be formed only by study of conditions and by securing all relevant information.

The teacher's business is to see that the occasion is taken advantage of. Since freedom resides in the operations of intelligent observation and judgment by which a purpose is developed, guidance given by the teacher to the exercise of the pupils' intelligence is an aid to freedom, not a restriction upon it. Sometimes teachers seem to be afraid even to make suggestions to the members of a group as to what they should do. I have heard of cases in which children are surrounded with objects and materials and then left entirely to themselves, the teacher being loath to suggest even what might be done with the materials lest freedom be infringed upon. Why, then, even supply materials, since they are a source of some suggestion or other? But what is more important is that the suggestion upon which pupils act must in any case come from somewhere. It is impossible to understand why a suggestion from one who has a larger experience and a wider horizon should not be at least as valid as a suggestion arising from some more or less accidental source.

It is possible of course to abuse the office, and to force the activity of the young into channels which express the teacher's purpose rather than that of the pupils. But the way to avoid this danger is not for the adult to withdraw entirely. The way is, first, for the teacher to be intelligently aware of the capacities, needs, and past experiences of those under instruction, and, secondly, to allow the suggestion made to develop into a plan and project by means of the further suggestions contributed and organized into a whole by the members of the group. The plan, in other words, is a co-operative enterprise, not a dictation. The teacher's suggestion is not a mold for a cast-iron result but is a starting point to be developed into a plan through contributions from the experience of all engaged in the learning process. The development occurs through reciprocal give-and-take, the teacher taking but not being afraid also to give. The essential point is that the purpose grow and take shape through the process of social intelligence.[4]

Selected Bibliography

ARCHAMBAULT, REGINALD D., ed. *Dewey on Education*. New York: Random House, 1966.

BOYDSTON, JO ANN, ed. *Guide to the Works of John Dewey*. Carbondale: Southern Illinois University Press, 1970.

CREMIN, LAWRENCE A. *The Transformation of the School: Progressivism in American Education, 1876-1957*. New York: Knopf, 1961.

GEIGER, GEORGE R. *John Dewey in Perspective*. New York: Oxford University Press, 1958.

SCHLIPP, PAUL A., ed. *The Philosophy of John Dewey*. Evanston: Northwestern University, 1939.

THOMAS, MILTON H. *John Dewey: A Centennial Bibliography*. Chicago: University of Chicago Press, 1962.

4. John Dewey, *Experience and Education* (New York: Macmillan, 1938), pp. 83-85. Used by permission of Kappa Delta Pi, an Honor Society in Education, owners of the copyright. Emphasis in the original.

8

Maria Montessori

Maria Montessori "achieved a universal reputation hardly second to Dewey's, and in the course of a long lifetime suffered, as he did, some misinterpretation by earnest disciples developing their own lines of thought."[1]

Montessori was born in Chiaravalle, Italy, on August 31, 1870. She graduated from the University of Rome with a degree in medicine in 1896, the first woman in Italy to earn this degree. Between 1898 and 1900 Montessori taught retarded children in the Orthophrenic School in Rome. Believing that her teaching methods would also be suitable for the education of normal children, she opened the first Children's House (Casa del Bambini) in 1907, for children from three to six years of age in a slum district of Rome. In 1909 she published *The Montessori Method,* which gives a basic statement of her views. Montessori devoted the remaining years of her life to the advancement of her ideas. She died on May 6, 1952, in Noordwijk-on-Sea, the Netherlands.

In the following selection, Montessori describes the basic elements in her method, which she calls the "method of observation." The role of the teacher (whom she calls a "directress") is a limited

1. S. J. Curtis and M. E. A. Boultwood, *A Short History of Educational Ideas,* 3rd ed. (London: University Tutorial Press, 1961), p. 496.

one, with the student learning through group and individual activities. Although Montessori states that her approach is based on "liberty," in actuality discipline is enforced by means of aversive techniques. Included in this selection is a description of the practices employed in the Children's Houses.

In the giving of . . . lessons the fundamental guide must be the *method of observation,* in which is included and understood the liberty of the child. So the teacher shall *observe* whether the child interests himself in the object, how he is interested in it, for how long, etc., even noticing the expression of his face. And she must take great care not to offend the principles of liberty. For, if she provokes the child to make an unnatural effort, she will no longer know what is the *spontaneous* activity of the child. If, therefore, the lesson rigorously prepared in this brevity, simplicity and truth is not understood by the child, is not accepted by him as an explanation of the object,—the teacher must be warned of two things:—first, not to *insist* by repeating the lesson; and second, *not to make the child feel that he has made a mistake,* or that he has not understood, because in doing so she will cause him to make an effort to understand, and will thus alter the natural state which must be used by her in making her psychological observation. . . .

We begin the day with a series of exercises of practical life, and I must confess that these exercises were the only part of the programme which proved thoroughly stationary. These exercises were such a success that they formed the beginning of the day in all of the "Children's Houses." . . .

As soon as the children arrive at school we make an inspection for cleanliness. If possible, this should be carried on in the presence of the mothers, but their attention should not be called to it directly. We examine the hands, the nails, the neck, the ears, the face, the teeth; and care is given to the tidiness of the hair. If any of the garments are torn or soiled or ripped, if the buttons are lacking, or if the shoes are not clean, we call the attention of the child to this. In this way, the children become accustomed to observing themselves and take an interest in their own appearance. . . .

After this care of their persons, we put on the little aprons. The children are able to put these on themselves, or, with the help of each other. Then we begin our visit about the schoolroom. We notice if all the various materials are in order and if they are clean. The teacher shows the children how to clean out the little corners where dust has accumulated, and shows them how to use the various objects necessary in cleaning a room,—dust-cloths, dust-brushes, little brooms, etc. All of this, when the children are allowed *to do it by themselves,* is very quickly accomplished. Then the children go each to his own place. The teacher explains to them that the normal position is for each child to be seated in his own place, in silence, with his feet together on the floor, his hands resting on the table, and his head erect. In this way she teaches them poise and equilibrium. Then she has them rise on their feet in order to sing the hymn, teaching them that in rising and sitting down it is not necessary to be noisy. In this way the children learn to move about the furniture with poise and with care. After this we have a series of exercises in which the children learn to move gracefully, to go and come, to salute each other, to lift objects carefully, to receive various objects from each other politely. The teacher calls attention with little exclamations to a child who is clean, a room which is well ordered, a class seated quietly, a graceful movement, etc.

From such a starting point we proceed to the free teaching. That is, the teacher will no longer make comments to the children, directing them how to move from their seats, etc., she will limit herself to correcting the disordered movements. . . .

The teacher moves quietly about, goes to any child who calls her, supervising operations in such a way that anyone who needs her finds her at his elbow, and whoever does not need her is not reminded of her existence. Sometimes, hours go by without a word. They seem "little men," as they were called by some visitors to the "Children's House"; or, as another suggested, "judges in deliberation."

In the midst of such intense interest in work it never happens that quarrels arise over the possession of an object. If one accomplishes something especially fine, his achievement is a source of admiration and joy to others: no heart suffers from another's wealth, but the triumph of one is a delight to all. Very often he finds ready imitators. They all seem happy and satisfied to do what they can, without feeling jealous of the deeds of others. The little fellow of three works peaceably beside the boy of seven, just as he is satisfied with his own height and does not envy the older boy's stature. Everything is growing in the most profound peace.

If the teacher wishes the whole assembly to do something, for instance, leave the work which interests them so much, all she needs to do is to speak a word in a low tone, or make a gesture, and they are all attention, they look toward her with eagerness, anxious to know how to obey. Many visitors have seen the teacher write orders on the blackboard, which were obeyed joyously by the children. Not only the teachers, but anyone who asks the pupils to do something is astonished to see them obey in the minutest detail and with obliging cheerfulness. Often a visitor wishes to hear how a child, now painting, can sing. The child leaves his painting to be obliging, but the instant his courteous action is completed, he returns to his interrupted work. Sometimes the smaller children finish their work before they obey. . . .

Discipline must come through liberty. Here is a great principle which is difficult for followers of common-school methods to understand. How shall one obtain *discipline* in a class of free children? . . .

If any educational act is to be efficacious, it will be only that which tends to *help* toward the complete unfolding of this life. To be thus helpful it is necessary rigorously to avoid the *arrest* of *spontaneous movements and the imposition of arbitrary tasks.* It is of course understood, that here we do not speak of useless or dangerous acts, for these must be *suppressed, destroyed.* . . .

As to punishments, we have many times come in contact with children who disturbed the others without paying any attention to our corrections. Such children were at once examined by the physician. When the case proved to be that of a normal child, we placed one of the little tables in a corner of the room, and in this way isolated the child; having him sit in a comfortable little armchair, so placed that he might see his companions at work, and giving him those games and toys to which he was most attracted. This isolation almost always succeeded in calming the child; from his position he could see the entire assembly of his companions, and the way in which they carried on their work was an *object lesson* much more efficacious than any words of the teacher could possibly have been. Little by little, he would come to see the advantages of being one of the company working so busily before his eyes, and he would really wish to go back and do as the others did. We have in this way led back again to discipline all the children who at first seemed to rebel against it. The isolated child was always made the object of special care, almost as if he were ill. I myself, when I entered the room, went first of all directly to him, caressing him, as if he were a very little child. Then I turned my attention to the others, interesting myself in their work, asking questions about it as if they had been little men. I do not know what happened in the soul of these children whom we found it necessary to discipline, but certainly the conversion was always very complete and lasting. They showed great pride in learning how to work and how to conduct themselves, and always showed a very tender affection for the teacher and for me. . . .

I have several *games* of *silence,* which help in a surprising way to strengthen the remarkable discipline of our children.

I call the children's attention to myself, telling them to see how silent I can be. I assume different positions; standing, sitting, and maintain each pose *silently, without movement.* A finger moving can produce a noise, even though it be imperceptible. We may breathe so that we may be heard. But I maintain *absolute* silence, which is not an easy thing to do. I call a child, and ask him to do as I am doing. He adjusts his feet to a better position, and this makes a noise! He moves an arm, stretching it out upon the arm of his chair; it is a noise. His breathing is not altogether silent, it is not tranquil, absolutely unheard as mine is.

During these manœuvres on the part of the child, and while my brief comments are followed by intervals of immobility and silence, the other children are watching and listening. Many of them are interested in the fact, which they have never noticed before; namely, that we make so many noises of which we are not conscious, and that there are *degrees* of *silence.* There is an absolute silence where nothing, *absolutely nothing* moves. They watch me in amazement when I stand in the middle of the room, so quietly that it is really as if "I were not." Then they strive to imitate me, and to do even better. I call attention here and there to a foot that moves, almost inadvertently. The attention of the child is called to every part of his body in an anxious eagerness to attain to immobility. . . .

"Now listen," we say. "A soft voice is going to call your name." Then going to a room behind the children, and standing within the open door, I call in a low voice, lingering over the syllables as if I were calling from across the mountains. This voice, almost occult, seems to reach the heart and to call to the soul of the child. Each one as he is called, lifts his head, opens his eyes as if altogether happy, then rises, silently seeking not to move the chair, and walks on the tips of his toes, so quietly that he is scarcely heard. Nevertheless his step resounds in the silence, and amid the immobility which persists.

Having reached the door, with a joyous face, he leaps into the room, choking back soft outbursts of laughter. Another child may come to hide his face against my dress, another, turning, will watch his companions sitting like statues silent and waiting. The one who is called feels that he is privileged, that he has received a gift, a prize. And yet they know that all will be called, "beginning with the most silent one in all the room." So each one tries to merit by his perfect silence the certain call. I once saw a little one of three years try to suffocate a sneeze, and succeed! She held her breath in her little breast, and resisted, coming out victorious. A most surprising effort!

This game delights the little ones beyond measure. Their intent faces, their patient immobility, reveal the enjoyment of a great pleasure. In the beginning, when the soul of the child was unknown to me, I had thought of showing them sweetmeats and little toys, promising to give them to the ones who were *called,* supposing that the gifts would be necessary to persuade the child to make the necessary effort. But I soon found that this was unnecessary.[2]

In the preceding excerpt Montessori's approach seems to exemplify the Exercise/Imitation Method. In the selection below, she explicitly recommends the use of didactic exercises, particu-

2. Maria Montessori, *The Montessori Method*, trans. Anne E. George (New York: Stokes, 1912) pp. 108-109, 121, 122, 122-23, 346-47, 86, 87-88, 103-104, 209-210, 210-11. Emphasis in the original.

larly for the education of the senses, but she also refers to "those
mental explosions which delight the child so intensely when he
makes discoveries." Therefore, Montessori's view of teaching
method appears to encompass both Exercise/Imitation and Dis-
covery/Restructuring. She further suggests that sensory training
might have a general improvement effect similar to that found in
the notion of mental discipline; her reference to "intellectual gym-
nastics" is, of course, reminiscent of Isocrates's "gymnastic of the
mind." The latter portion of the excerpt illustrates specific applications of her technique.

> It is exactly in the repetition of the exercises that
> the education of the senses consists; their aim is not that the
> child shall *know* colours, forms and the different qualities
> of objects, but that he refine his senses through an exercise
> of attention, of comparison, of judgment. These exercises are
> true intellectual gymnastics. Such gymnastics, reasonably
> directed by means of various devices, aid in the formation
> of the intellect, just as physical exercises fortify the general
> health and quicken the growth of the body. The child who
> trains his various senses separately, by means of external
> stimuli, concentrates his attention and develops, piece by
> piece, his mental activities, just as with separately prepared
> movements he trains his muscular activities. These mental
> gymnastics are not merely psycho-sensory, but they prepare
> the way for spontaneous association of ideas, for ratiocina-
> tion developing out of definite knowledge, for a harmonious-
> ly balanced intellect. They are the powder-trains that bring
> about those mental explosions which delight the child so
> intensely when he makes discoveries in the world about him,
> when he, at the same time, ponders over and glories in the
> new things which are revealed to him in the outside world,
> and in the exquisite emotions of his own growing conscious-
> ness; and finally when there spring up within him, almost
> by a process of spontaneous ripening, like the internal phe-
> nomena of growth, the external products of learning—writ-
> ing and reading. . . .
> Our children have . . . among the didactic material for
> the education of the senses, a series of ten cubes. The first
> has a base of ten centimetres, and the others decrease, suc-
> cessively, one centimetre as to base, the smallest cube having

a base of one centimetre. The exercise consists in throwing the blocks, which are pink in colour, down upon a green carpet, and then building them up into a little tower, placing the largest cube as the base, and then placing the others in order of size until the little cube of one centimetre is placed at the top.

The little one must each time select, from the blocks scattered upon the green carpet, "the largest" block. This game is most entertaining to the little ones of two years and a half, who, as soon as they have constructed the little tower, tumble it down with little blows of the hand, admiring the pink cubes as they lie scattered upon the green carpet. Then, they begin again the construction, building and destroying a definite number of times. . . .

In conclusion, let me summarize briefly: Our didactic material renders auto-education possible, permits a methodical education of the senses. Not upon the ability of the teacher does such education rest, but upon the didactic system. This presents objects which, first, attract the spontaneous attention of the child, and, second, contain a rational gradation of stimuli. . . .

However desirable it may be to furnish a sense education as a basis for intellectual ideas, it is nevertheless advisable at the same time to associate the *language* with these *perceptions*. . . .

First Period.   The association of the sensory perception with the name.

For example, we present to the child, two colours, red and blue. Presenting the red, we say simply, "This is red," and presenting the blue, "This is blue." Then, we lay the spools upon the table under the eyes of the child.

Second Period.   Recognition of the object corresponding to the name. We say to the child, "Give me the red," and then, "Give me the blue."

Third Period.   The remembering of the name corresponding to the object. We ask the child, showing him the object, "What is this?" and he should respond, "Red." . . .

The education of the tactile and the thermic senses go together, since the warm bath, and heat in general, render the tactile sense more acute. Since to exercise the tactile sense it is necessary to *touch*, bathing the hands in warm water has the additional advantage of teaching the child a principle of cleanliness—that of not touching objects with hands that are not clean. I therefore apply the general notions of practical life, regarding the washing of the hands, care of the nails, to the exercises preparatory to the discrimination of tactile stimuli.

The limitation of the exercises of the tactile sense to the cushioned tips of the fingers, is rendered necessary by practical life. It must be made a necessary phase of *education* because it prepares for a life in which man exercises and uses the tactile sense through the medium of these finger tips. Hence,I have the child wash his hands carefully with soap, in a little basin; and in another basin I have him rinse them in a bath of tepid water. Then I show him how to dry and rub his hands gently, in this way preparing for the regular bath. I next teach the child how to *touch,* that is, the manner in which he should touch surfaces. For this it is necessary to take the finger of the child and to draw *it very, very lightly* over the surface.

Another particular of the technique is to teach the child to hold his eyes closed while he touches, encouraging him to do this by telling him that he will be able to feel the differences better, and so leading him to distinguish, without the help of sight, the change of contact. He will quickly learn, and will show that he enjoys the exercise. Often after the introduction of such exercises, it is a common thing to have a child come to you, and, closing his eyes, touch with great delicacy the palm of your hand or the cloth of your dress, especially any silken or velvet trimmings. They do verily *exercise* the tactile sense. They enjoy keenly touching any soft pleasant surface, and become exceedingly keen in discriminating between the differences in the sandpaper cards.[3]

Selected Bibliography

BOYD, WILLIAM. *From Locke to Montessori: A Critical Account of the Montessori Point of View.* London: Harrap, 1914.

KILPATRICK, WILLIAM H. *The Montessori System Examined.* Boston: Houghton Mifflin, 1914.

3. *Ibid.,* pp. 360-61, 174, 174-75, 177, 177-78, 185-86. Emphasis in the original.

Maria Montessori: A Centenary Anthology, 1870-1970. Amsterdam: Association Montessori Internationale, 1970.

STANDING, E. MORTIMER. *Maria Montessori: Her Life and Work.* Fresno, Calif.: American Library Guild, 1959.

9

Edward L. Thorndike
and B. F. Skinner

In this chapter we shall jointly consider Edward L. Thorndike and Burrhus F. Skinner, since both men have contributed to the development of the fifth (and last) major view on instructional method in our classification. We have called this the Reinforcement Method. The essential feature of this method is the deliberate use of post-response outcome-shaping stimuli. Although teachers have probably unknowingly made use of this method for thousands of years, it was not until psychologists began their scientific study of the learning process that the role of these stimuli as a factor in learning was explicitly recognized. The effort-producing stimuli used with the Reinforcement Method may either be overtly provided, aversive stimuli or student-originated stimuli.

Although the use of post-response outcome-shaping stimuli is the basic characteristic of the Reinforcement Method, this method ordinarily involves the use of pre-response outcome-shaping stimuli in a way that is similar to their use in the Exercise/Imitation Method or the Discovery/Restructuring method. For example, a teacher may praise a student for correctly performing a required exercise or for being able to discover the solution to a problem that has been presented by the teacher. In these illustrations the exercise or the problem would constitute pre-response outcome-shaping stimuli, while the word of praise would be the reinforcement.

Thorndike contributed to the development of the Reinforcement Method by being the first person to recognize explicitly the relationship between reinforcement and learning. He was born on August 31, 1874, in Williamsburg, Massachusetts. He graduated with a bachelor's degree from Wesleyan University in 1895 and received a Ph.D. degree in psychology from Columbia University in 1898. Thorndike then took a position as a teacher of education in the College for Women of Western Reserve University. One year later, in 1899, he moved to Teachers College, Columbia University, where he became professor of educational psychology. Thorndike published many works in the fields of psychology and education; among his educational writings is *Education: A First Book* (1912). Thorndike retired from Teachers College in 1940; he died in Montrose, New York, on August 9, 1949.

Thorndike described the use of reinforcement as the "Law of Effect." In the following selection Thorndike states the law and indicates how it can be applied to teaching.

The Law of Effect is that, other things being equal, *the greater the satisfyingness of the state of affairs which accompanies or follows a given response to a certain situation, the more likely that response is to be made to that situation in the future.* Conversely, the greater the discomfort or annoyingness of the state of affairs which comes with or after a response to a situation, the more likely that response is *not* to be made to that situation in the future. Suppose, for example, that when a child responds to the situation, *being asked, "How many are four and two?,"* by saying "Six," he is always given kind looks, candy and the approval of his fellows. Suppose, on the contrary, that he always received rebukes, blows and jeers. This law may be stated more briefly as:—*Satisfying results strengthen, and discomfort weakens, the bond between situation and response.*

Old connections between situation and response are weakened, and new connections are created, only by some force. Human nature does not do something for nothing. The satisfyingness and annoyingness of the states of affairs which follow the making of the connection are the chief forces which remodel man's nature. Education makes changes chiefly by rewarding them. The prime law in all human control is to get the man to make the desired response and to be satisfied thereby.

The Law of Effect is the fundamental law of learning and teaching. By it a crab learns to respond to the situation, *two paths*, by taking the one, choice of which has in the past brought food. By it a dog will learn to respond to the situation, *a white box and a black box*, by neglecting the latter if opening it in the past has been promptly followed by an electric shock. By it animals are taught their tricks; by it babies learn to smile at the sight of the bottle or the kind attendant, and to manipulate spoon and fork; by it the player at billiards or golf improves his game; by it the man of science preserves those ideas that satisfy him by their promise, and discards futile fancies. It is the great weapon of all who wish—in industry, trade, government, religion or education—to change men's responses, either by reinforcing old and adding new ones, or by getting rid of those that are undesirable.[1]

Thorndike later modified his conception of the Law of Effect. Instead of regarding pleasant and unpleasant consequences as having equal effect, he identified satisfiers as being of primary importance in the reinforcement of learning.

Annoyers do not act on learning in general by weakening whatever connection they follow. If they do anything to learning they do it indirectly by informing the learner that such and such a response in such and such a situation brings distress, or by making the learner feel fear of a certain object, or by making him jump back from a certain place, or by some other definite and specific change which they produce in him. Satisfiers *seem* to act more directly and generally and uniformly and subtly, but just what they do should be studied with much more care than anybody has yet devoted to it.[2]

1. Edward L. Thorndike, *Education: A First Book* (New York: Macmillan, 1912), pp. 96-97. Emphasis in the original.
2. Edward L. Thorndike, *Human Learning* (New York: Century, 1931), p. 46. Emphasis in the original.

Unfortunately, Thorndike did not elaborate the implications of his Law of Effect for teaching practice. But another psychologist, B. F. Skinner, has supplied us with a comprehensive statement of how reinforcement may be applied in the classroom.[3] Skinner was born in Susquehanna, Pennsylvania, on March 20, 1904. He earned a bachelor's degree from Hamilton College in 1926 and a Ph.D. degree from Harvard University in 1931. Skinner served as a professor of psychology at the University of Minnesota (1936-1945), Indiana University (1945-1948), and from 1948 to the present at Harvard University. The major statement of his educational views is *The Technology of Teaching* (1968).[4] The following selection, which also appears in Chapter 2 of *The Technology of Teaching*, summarizes the main points of Skinner's view.

Some promising advances have recently been made in the field of learning. Special techniques have been designed to arrange what are called "contingencies of reinforcement"—the relations which prevail between behavior on the one hand and the consequences of that behavior on the other—with the result that a much more effective control of behavior has been achieved. . . .

The Law of Effect has been taken seriously; we have made sure that effects *do* occur and that they occur under conditions which are optimal for producing the changes called learning. Once we have arranged the particular type of consequence called a reinforcement, our techniques permit us to shape up the behavior of an organism almost at will. It has become a routine exercise to demonstrate this in classes in elementary psychology by conditioning such an organism as a pigeon. Simply by presenting food to a hungry pigeon at the right time, it is possible to shape up three or four well-defined responses in a single demonstration period —such responses as turning around, pacing the floor in the

3. Although Skinner did not work with Thorndike, he has recognized Thorndike's influence and acknowledged that his ideas are an elaboration of Thorndike's earlier views. See Geraldine Joncich, *The Sane Positivist: A Biography of Edward L. Thorndike* (Middletown, Conn.: Wesleyan University Press, 1968), p. 506.

4. B. F. Skinner, *The Technology of Teaching* (New York: Appleton-Century-Crofts, 1968).

pattern of a figure-8, standing still in a corner of the demonstration apparatus, stretching the neck, or stamping the foot.
Extremely complex performances may be reached through
successive stages in the shaping process, the contingencies
of reinforcement being changed progressively in the direction of the required behavior. The results are often quite
dramatic. In such a demonstration one can *see* learning take
place. A significant change in behavior is often obvious as
the result of a single reinforcement. . . .

From this exciting prospect of an advancing science of
learning, it is a great shock to turn to that branch of technology which is most directly concerned with the learning
process—education. Let us consider, for example, the teaching of arithmetic in the lower grades. The school is concerned with imparting to the child a large number of responses of a special sort. The responses are all verbal. They
consist of speaking and writing certain words, figures, and
signs which, to put it roughly, refer to numbers and to arithmetic operations. The first task is to shape up these responses
—to get the child to pronounce and to write responses correctly, but the principal task is to bring this behavior under
many sorts of stimulus control. This is what happens when
the child learns to count, to recite tables, to count while tick-
ing off the items in an assemblage of objects, to respond to
spoken or written numbers by saying "odd," "even," "prime,"
and so on. Over and above this elaborate repertoire of numerical behavior, most of which is often dismissed as the
product of rote learning, the teaching of arithmetic looks
forward to those complex serial arrangements of responses
involved in original mathematical thinking. The child must
acquire responses of transposing, clearing fractions, and so
on, which modify the order or pattern of the original material so that the response called a solution is eventually
made possible.

Now, how is this extremely complicated verbal repertoire set up? In the first place, what reinforcements are used?
Fifty years ago the answer would have been clear. At that
time educational control was still frankly aversive. The child
read numbers, copied numbers, memorized tables, and performed operations upon numbers to escape the threat of the
birch rod or cane. Some positive reinforcements were perhaps eventually derived from the increased efficiency of the
child in the field of arithmetic and in rare cases some auto-

matic reinforcement may have resulted from the sheer manipulation of the medium—from the solution of problems or the discovery of the intricacies of the number system. But for the immediate purposes of education the child acted to avoid or escape punishment. It was part of the reform movement known as progressive education to make the positive consequences more immediately effective, but any one who visits the lower grades of the average school today will observe that a change has been made, not from aversive to positive control, but from one form of aversive stimulation to another. The child at his desk, filling in his workbook, is behaving primarily to escape from the threat of a series of minor aversive events—the teacher's displeasure, the criticism or ridicule of his classmates, an ignominious showing in a competition, low marks, a trip to the office "to be talked to" by the principal, or a word to the parent who may still resort to the birch rod. In this welter of aversive consequences, getting the right answer is in itself an insignificant event, any effect of which is lost amid the anxieties, the boredom, and the aggressions which are the inevitable by-products of aversive control.

Secondly, we have to ask how the contingencies of reinforcement are arranged. When is a numerical operation reinforced as "right"? Eventually, of course, the pupil may be able to check his own answers and achieve some sort of automatic reinforcement, but in the early stages the reinforcement of being right is usually accorded by the teacher. The contingencies she provides are far from optimal. It can easily be demonstrated that, unless explicit mediating behavior has been set up, the lapse of only a few seconds between response and reinforcement destroys most of the effect. In a typical classroom, nevertheless, long periods of time customarily elapse. The teacher may walk up and down the aisle, for example, while the class is working on a sheet of problems, pausing here and there to say right or wrong. Many seconds or minutes intervene between the child's response and the teacher's reinforcement. In many cases—for example, when papers are taken home to be corrected—as much as 24 hours may intervene. It is surprising that this system has any effect whatsoever.

A third notable shortcoming is the lack of a skillful program which moves forward through a series of progressive approximations to the final complex behavior desired. A long series of contingencies is necessary to bring the organism into the possession of mathematical behavior most efficiently. But the teacher is seldom able to reinforce at each step in such a series because she cannot deal with the pupil's responses one at a time. It is usually necessary to reinforce the behavior in blocks of responses—as in correcting a work sheet or page from a workbook. The responses within such a block must not be interrelated. The answer to one problem must not depend upon the answer to another. The number of stages through which one may progressively approach a complex pattern of behavior is therefore small, and the task so much the more difficult. Even the most modern workbook in beginning arithmetic is far from exemplifying an efficient program for shaping up mathematical behavior.

Perhaps the most serious criticism of the current classroom is the relative infrequency of reinforcement. Since the pupil is usually dependent upon the teacher for being right, and since many pupils are usually dependent upon the same teacher, the total number of contingencies which may be arranged during, say, the first four years, is of the order of only a few thousand. But a very rough estimate suggests that efficient mathematical behavior at this level requires something of the order of 25,000 contingencies. We may suppose that even in the brighter student a given contingency must be arranged several times to place the behavior well in hand. The responses to be set up are not simply the various items in tables of addition, subtraction, multiplication, and division; we have also to consider the alternative forms in which each item may be stated. To the learning of such material we should add hundreds of responses concerned with factoring, identifying primes, memorizing series, using short-cut techniques of calculation, constructing and using geometric representations or number forms, and so on. Over and above all this, the whole mathematical repertoire must be brought under the control of concrete problems of considerable variety. Perhaps 50,000 contingencies is a more conservative estimate. In this frame of reference the daily assignment in arithmetic seems pitifully meagre.

The result of all this is, of course, well known. Even our best schools are under criticism for their inefficiency in the teaching of drill subjects such as arithmetic. The condition in the average school is a matter of wide-spread national concern. Modern children simply do not learn arithmetic quickly or well. . . .

There would be no point in urging these objections if improvement were impossible. But the advances which have recently been made in our control of the learning process suggest a thorough revision of classroom practices and, fortunately, they tell us how the revision can be brought about. This is not, of course, the first time that the results of an experimental science have been brought to bear upon the practical problems of education. The modern classroom does not, however, offer much evidence that research in the field of learning has been respected or used. This condition is no doubt partly due to the limitations of earlier research. But it has been encouraged by a too hasty conclusion that the laboratory study of learning is inherently limited because it cannot take into account the realities of the classroom. In the light of our increasing knowledge of the learning process we should, instead, insist upon dealing with those realities and forcing a substantial change in them. Education is perhaps the most important branch of scientific technology. It deeply affects the lives of all of us. We can no longer allow the exigencies of a practical situation to suppress the tremendous improvements which are within reach. The practical situation must be changed.

There are certain questions which have to be answered in turning to the study of any new organism. What behavior is to be set up? What reinforcers are at hand? What responses are available in embarking upon a program of progressive approximation which will lead to the final form of the behavior? How can reinforcements be most efficiently scheduled to maintain the behavior in strength? These questions are all relevant in considering the problem of the child in the lower grades.

In the first place, what reinforcements are available? What does the school have in its possession which will reinforce a child? We may look first to the material to be learned, for it is possible that this will provide considerable automatic reinforcement. Children play for hours with mechanical toys, paints, scissors and paper, noise-makers, puzzles—in short, with almost anything which feeds back significant changes in the environment and is reasonably free of aversive properties. The sheer control of nature is itself reinforcing. This effect is not evident in the modern school because it is masked by the emotional responses generated by aversive control. It is true that automatic reinforcement from the manipulation of the environment is probably only a mild reinforcer and may need to be carefully husbanded, but one of the most striking principles to emerge from recent research is that the *net* amount of reinforcement is of little significance. A very slight reinforcement may be tremendously effective in controlling behavior if it is wisely used.

If the natural reinforcement inherent in the subject matter is not enough, other reinforcers must be employed. Even in school the child is occasionally permitted to do "what he wants to do," and access to reinforcements of many sorts may be made contingent upon the more immediate consequences of the behavior to be established. Those who advocate competition as a useful social motive may wish to use the reinforcements which follow from excelling others, although there is the difficulty that in this case the reinforcement of one child is necessarily aversive to another. Next in order we might place the good will and affection of the teacher, and only when that has failed need we turn to the use of aversive stimulation.

In the second place, how are these reinforcements to be made contingent upon the desired behavior? There are two considerations here—the gradual elaboration of extremely complex patterns of behavior and the maintenance of the behavior in strength at each stage. The whole process of becoming competent in any field must be divided into a very large number of very small steps, and reinforcement must be contingent upon the accomplishment of each step. This solution to the problem of creating a complex repertoire of behavior also solves the problem of maintaining the behavior in strength. We could, of course, resort to the techniques of scheduling already developed in the study of other organisms but in the present state of our knowledge of educational practices, scheduling appears to be most effectively arranged through the design of the material to be learned. By making each successive step as small as possible, the frequency of reinforcement can be raised to a maximum, while the possibly aversive consequences of being wrong are reduced to a minimum. Other ways of designing material would yield other programs of reinforcement. Any supplementary reinforcement would probably have to be scheduled in the more traditional way.

These requirements are not excessive, but they are probably incompatible with the current realities of the classroom. In the experimental study of learning it has been found that the contingencies of reinforcement which are most efficient in controlling the organism cannot be arranged through the personal mediation of the experimenter. An organism is affected by subtle details of contingencies which are beyond the capacity of the human organism to arrange. Mechnical and electrical devices must be used. Mechanical help is also demanded by the sheer number of contingencies which may be used efficiently in a single experimental session. We have recorded many millions of responses from a single organism during thousands of experimental hours. Personal arrangement of the contingencies and personal observation of the results are quite unthinkable. Now, the human organism is, if anything, more sensitive to precise contingencies than the other organisms we have studied. We have every reason to expect, therefore, that the most effective control of human learning will require instrumental aid. The simple fact is that, as a mere reinforcing mechanism, the teacher is out of date. This would be true even if a single teacher devoted all her time to a single child, but her inadequacy is multiplied many-fold when she must serve as a reinforcing device to many children at once. If the teacher is to take advantage of recent advances in the study of learning, she must have the help of mechanical devices.[5]

Selected Bibliography

Evans, Richard I. *B. F. Skinner:The Man and His Ideas.* New York: Dutton, 1968.

Joncich, Geraldine, ed. *Psychology and the Science of Education: Selected Writings of Edward L. Thorndike.* New York: Bureau of Publications, Teachers College, Columbia University, 1962.

5. B. F. Skinner, "The Science of Learning and the Art of Teaching," *Harvard Educational Review* 24 (Spring 1954): 86, 86-87, 90-92, 93-95. Copyright 1954 by President and Fellows of Harvard College. Reprinted with permission. Emphasis in the original.

JONCICH, GERALDINE. *The Sane Positivist: A Biography of Edward L. Thorndike*. Middletown, Conn.: Wesleyan University Press, 1968.

POSTMAN, LEO. "The History and Present Status of the Law of Effect." *Psychological Bulletin* 44 (1947):489-563.

10

Concluding
Observations

In Chapter 1 we raised the question "How many fundamentally different methods of teaching have been devised, and what are the characteristics of the basic teaching methods?" Using the criteria for the classification of teaching methods that we proposed in the first chapter, we found that the major Western educational writers have advocated five fundamentally different approaches to teaching, three of which were developed before or during the Greco-Roman period and the last two of which were formulated since 1750. In this chapter we shall offer some concluding comments and observations.

Present Status of Views
on Teaching Method

Have any of the five conceptions of teaching method been rejected by contemporary teachers or is each of these views relevant today? Even a cursory examination of the present-day approaches to teaching method reveals that all five conceptions are still considered to be important.

Telling/Showing Method. This method occupies an important place in the conduct of schooling. It is probably the most widely used technique for education at the university level and of considerable significance in teaching at the secondary and primary levels. The Telling/Showing Method is also involved in some of the modern innovations in teaching practice. For example, televised instruction relies primarily on the Telling/Showing Method.

Exercise/Imitation Method. This teaching method also has a central role in modern educational practice. It is found, for example, in the teaching of most skills (for example, reading, writing, and arithmetic skills at the primary and secondary levels, and in professional-vocational training at the higher education level). It is, of course, the method usually involved in the study activities of students outside of class, particularly in their preparation for examinations. A major emphasis in contemporary attempts to improve the Exercise/Imitation Method involves the provision of better feedback to the student concerning his learning performances, which is exemplified in what is commonly referred to as "micro-teaching."

Discovery/Restructuring Method. Of the three traditional methods of instruction, the Discovery/Restructuring Method has received the greatest amount of attention from contemporary educational thinkers. Jean Piaget, the eminent Swiss psychologist, has argued that "teaching means creating situations where structures can be discovered; it does not mean transmitting structures which may be assimilated at nothing other than a verbal level."[1] Another present-day advocate of the Discovery/Restructuring Method is Jerome Bruner, also a noted psychologist. In his view the school "is primarily the special community where one experiences discovery by the use of intelligence, where one leaps into new and unimagined realms of experience, experience that is discontinuous with what went before."[2]

The Discovery/Restructuring Method is extensively used today by teachers in various classes, but particularly in mathematics and science. And, of course, many contemporary discussion tech-

1. Quoted in Charles E. Silberman, *Crisis in the Classroom* (New York: Vintage Books, 1971), p. 218.
2. Jerome S. Bruner, *On Knowing: Essays for the Left Hand* (Cambridge, Mass.: Harvard University Press, 1962), p. 118.

niques and questioning strategies follow the example of Socrates and reflect this method.

Student Interest Method. A number of present-day education writers have committed themselves to the Student Interest Method. Typical of this group of writers is A. S. Neill, the founder of the Summerhill school in England: "We have no new methods of teaching, because we do not consider that teaching in itself matters very much. Whether a school has or has not a special method for teaching long division is of no significance, for long division is of no importance except to those who *want* to learn it. And the child who *wants* to learn long division *will* learn it no matter how it is taught."[3] Another advocate of the Student Interest Method is Herbert Kohl: "The role of the teacher is not to control his pupils but rather to enable them to make choices and pursue what interests them."[4] Paul Goodman has written as follows: "We can, I believe, educate the young entirely in terms of their free choice, with no processing whatever. Nothing can be efficiently learned, or, indeed, learned at all—other than through parroting or brute training, when acquired knowledge is promptly forgotten after the examination—unless it meets need, desire, curiosity, or fantasy."[5] Finally, John Holt has offered the following view: "I think children learn better when they learn what they want to learn when they want to learn it, and how they want to learn it, learning for their own curiosity and not at somebody else's order."[6]

Reinforcement Method. The Reinforcement Method, which is itself a twentieth century development in instructional method, has been popularized in two major forms: programmed instruction and "behavior modification." Programmed instruction provides the student (by means of a mechanical device or book) with a specially arranged sequence of material to be learned. The material is presented in a question-response manner such that the student will almost always give the correct response to the ques-

3. A. S. Neill, *Summerhill* (New York: Hart, 1960), p. 5. Emphasis in the original.
4. Herbert R. Kohl, *The Open Classroom* (New York: The New York Review, 1969), p. 20.
5. Paul Goodman, "No Processing Whatever," *Radical School Reform*, ed. Beatrice and Ronald Gross (New York: Simon and Schuster, 1969), p. 99.
6. John Holt, *The Underachieving School* (New York: Dell, 1970), p. 204.

tion or problem posed. When the student makes a correct response he is immediately reinforced through knowledge of his success.

The behavior modification approach, in its classroom application, utilizes the teacher as the dispenser of reinforcement. The key to this technique is that the teacher must be aware of the nature of the reinforcement process and act accordingly. Thus approved student behaviors may be rewarded by appropriate words, gestures, tokens, and prizes, while non-approved behaviors are not recognized.[7]

Prospects for a Sixth Teaching Method

What are the prospects for a sixth basic conception of teaching method? Considering that only two new views of teaching method have been developed since the Greco-Roman period, it would seem that a sixth fundamentally different approach to teaching may be difficult to formulate.

If a sixth conception is to be produced, we believe that it will most likely derive from a new theory of learning. Perhaps the recent experimentation on the "chemistry of learning," which suggests that learning involves chemical changes in the brain, will enable teachers to give students specially prepared pills that will produce the desired learning outcome through direct chemical means.[8] If such a procedure is eventually incorporated into teaching practice, then mankind will have created another basic teaching method.

In the meantime, we can continue our efforts to improve the utilization of the existing basic teaching methods. The major prospect for improvement, we believe, is in the *selection* of pre-response outcome-shaping stimuli. Except for the Reinforcement Method, all teaching methods require pre-response outcome-shaping stimuli; and most applications of the Reinforcement

---

7. For further information on this approach, see George A. Fargo, Charlene Behrns, and Patricia Nolen, eds., *Behavior Modification in the Classroom* (Belmont, Calif.: Wadsworth, 1970); and K. Daniel O'Leary and Susan G. O'Leary, *Classroom Management: The Successful Use of Behavioral Modification* (New York: Pergamon Press, 1972).

8. See Karl H. Pribram, ed., *On the Biology of Learning* (New York: Harcourt, Brace and World, 1969).

Method do, in fact, entail the use of pre-response as well as post-response outcome-shaping stimuli. Since pre-response outcome-shaping stimuli may vary in many respects (for example, qualitatively and in their intensity, frequency and sequence of presentation), and since different stimuli may be required to attain a given result with different kinds of students, the determination of the most appropriate stimuli for a particular teaching situation may be controversial. In fact, many or perhaps most present-day controversies over teaching method do not involve a choice between basic methods; instead, these controversies reflect different points of view regarding the appropriate use of pre-response outcome-shaping stimuli within a given teaching method. For example: the argument over whether reading taught by means of a phonics approach or the "look-say" approach represents the better selection of pre-response outcome-shaping stimuli.

We are fortunate, however, in that research on the teaching-learning process can help us to find out which pre-response outcome-shaping stimuli are the most effective for reaching stipulated learning objectives with different types of students. Therefore, we may anticipate that in the future some or all of the controversies concerning outcome-shaping stimuli will be resolved. Even if it should be a very long time before another new basic teaching method is formulated, we can at least expect considerable improvement in the use of the teaching methods we already have.